"In their new book, *Li(*
dell offer a powerful *
ing to honor God witl
approach, combined with biblically anchored wisdom,
provides invaluable insights for every man. If you strive to
live with faith, courage, and spiritual purpose, this book
is for you."

Craig Groeschel, founding and senior pastor,
Life.Church, *New York Times* bestselling author

"*Lionhearted* is a book men need to read. With biblical
clarity and conviction, David and Brandon Lindell guide
you toward a life that rises to the level of your God-given
purpose. If you desire to live focused, fulfilled, and fearless, this book is for you!"

Kirk Cousins, quarterback, Atlanta Falcons,
author of *Game Changer*

"*Lionhearted* by David and Brandon Lindell is a powerful
call to action for men seeking a life of purpose and
strength. This book challenges you to embrace the intentionality and courage of a lion, transforming your heart
and life with Christ's guidance. For those ready to make a
meaningful change, *Lionhearted* offers the insight and inspiration needed to live with true focus and fearlessness."

Chad Veach, lead pastor, Zoe Church,
author and international speaker

"David and Brandon Lindell are committed and creative leaders with vision. Their book, *Lionhearted*, speaks to the soul and draws out the courage in every man. You will be encouraged and challenged as the enemy's plots are exposed and the heart of God for every man is revealed. Purpose will be ignited as you are reminded of who God created you to be!"

Rich Wilkerson Jr., lead pastor, Vous Church, author of *Single & Secure*, *Friend of Sinners*, and *Sandcastle Kings*

"There's nothing tame about *Lionhearted*—this book is sure to awaken the passion, purpose, and power God has placed within every man! David and Brandon Lindell understand firsthand the various challenges faced by the next generation of husbands, fathers, sons, and brothers. They also know the path forward can be found in the timeless truth of God's Word and the ultimate example of manhood—Jesus Christ. *Lionhearted* is for anyone who wants to unleash his full potential."

Chris Hodges, senior pastor, Church of the Highlands, author of *Out of the Cave* and *Pray First*

"Every man wants to know how to live lionhearted. In this phenomenal book full of the truth of God's Word, David and Brandon tell us how."

Josh Hawley, senator of Missouri, author of *Manhood: The Masculine Virtues America Needs*

LIONHEARTED

LIONHEARTED

A MAN'S GUIDE TO LIVING
FOCUSED, FULFILLED & FEARLESS

DAVID LINDELL
and BRANDON LINDELL

R
Revell
a division of Baker Publishing Group
Grand Rapids, Michigan

Published by Revell
a division of Baker Publishing Group
Grand Rapids, Michigan
RevellBooks.com

Printed in the United States of America

Library of Congress Cataloging-in-Publication Data
Names: Lindell, David, author. | Lindell, Brandon, author.
Title: Lionhearted : a man's guide to living focused, fulfilled, and fearless / David Lindell and Brandon Lindell.
Description: Grand Rapids, Michigan : Revell, a division of Baker Publishing Group, [2025] | Includes bibliographical references.
Identifiers: LCCN 2024039377 | ISBN 9780800746247 (paperback) | ISBN 9780800746865 (casebound) | ISBN 9781493448753 (ebook)
Subjects: LCSH: Christian men—Religious life—Biblical teaching. | Heart—Religious aspects—Christianity.
Classification: LCC BV4528.2 .L56 2025 | DDC 248.8/42—dc23/eng/20241108
LC record available at https://lccn.loc.gov/2024039377

Design and illustration by Nathanael Burks and Josiah Hartmann

Baker Publishing Group publications use paper produced from sustainable forestry practices and postconsumer waste whenever possible.

25 26 27 28 29 30 31   7 6 5 4 3 2 1

For the lionhearted men in our lives:

Our grandpas,
Donald Lindell and Timothy Keene
&
Our dad,
John Lindell

CONTENTS

PART 3 The Lionhearted Life

FOREWORD

It is an unsettling thing to look directly into the eyes of a lion. In that moment, you understand exactly why they earned their spot at the top of the food chain. Lions are apex predators. This means they hunt what they want but are never hunted by any other animal. They can run fifty miles per hour and jump up to thirty-six feet in a single bound. The roar of a lion can be heard from five miles away and can reach up to 114 decibels. Somehow, you can feel all that power when you lock eyes with one, whether at a zoo, on a safari, or even in a photo. It taps into a primitive part of you, making you grateful for the glass or cage that separates you and keeps you safe.

My family and I were in South Africa once, and after striking out on lions during our game drives, we took a "your car is your cage" drive through a lion park where you were guaranteed to get close to Simba, Mufasa, Nala, and even Scar. I was sitting in the back seat of the minivan and had been told no less than ten times not to open the door or window while in the lion enclosure because the lions roamed free and were known to pounce when a door opened. After googling and discovering there had been tourist fatalities, I became very aware of how close my knee was to the button that would open the door as we passed close enough to see the lions' muscles ripple and the plaque on their teeth when they yawned. I pictured myself accidentally clicking it and desperately trying to close it before we all became an American snack.

I left the experience with a profound respect for the king of the jungle and a new awareness of the incredible compliment it is that God, in His kindness, wants to make us like lions (Proverbs 28:1). That is the heartbeat of the book you are holding in your hands: that you, as a man, would tap into the boldness of the Lion of the tribe of Judah. Today, the power and design of manhood is misunderstood, forgotten, and often seen as something to be ashamed of.

The devil opposes manhood because he is terrified of it. He knows that when you tap into the lionhearted life God is calling you to, there is a roar waiting to be unleashed. This doesn't mean you will be a brute. Lions have retractable claws, and real men can use theirs when needed, but put them away when gentleness is required.

Don't be discouraged if that feels a million miles from where you are today. As amazing as the eyes of a lion become later in life, it is incredible to know that lions are born blind. They go on to develop incredible night vision, which my friends Brandon and David will explain in detail in chapter 8, but they start out unable to see anything at all. This should give you hope. Because according to

Jesus, the true Lion King, the first step toward seeing is to admit you are blind (John 9:41). So take a breath, admit that you need God's help to tap into the focused, fulfilled, and fearless life Jesus died for you to have, and then buckle your seat belt before you turn the page—because this will be a wild ride.

Levi Lusko, bestselling author of
Through the Eyes of a Lion

INTRODUCTION

Adventure awaits.

We love the mountains. There is something soul-stirring about being surrounded by peaks, spires, and cliff faces towering thousands of feet above you. They stop you in your tracks, seizing you with wonder, while simultaneously compelling you to grab your CamelBak and hit the trail.

When we were growing up, our family made regular pilgrimages to Rocky Mountain National Park, and every time we entered, we immediately started scoping out all the rocks we wanted to climb. Now, it's important you understand that neither of us has ever qualified as mountaineers or even climbers in any technical sense, but what we lacked in skill was made up for in imagination. We could see ourselves ascending. From our vantage point in the back seat of the car, every rock we saw was a rock we could definitely climb if our parents would only turn us loose on the mountainside.

Now we are parents, and though our families love the national parks, our perspective has shifted. You could say that we have developed a healthier respect for the journey. Our own kids are now the ones clamoring to be released and go explore. And it's not that our sense of adventure has vanished, but we have discovered that the route you take matters. Even the best climbers in the world know this to be true. Just watch Alex Honnold's nail-biting, rope-less ascent up the three-thousand-foot face of El Capitan, documented in the film *Free Solo* (if you haven't watched it, that should be one of the first things you do at the start of your journey through this book). Alex chooses his way very carefully. He climbs along established routes. Haphazard exploration at such great heights can easily prove deadly.

In many ways, this is what this entire book is about. Every man is hardwired with the desire for adventure—uncharted territory, new challenges, unexplored vistas. We are made for a lionhearted existence. The issue is how to get there—because the route you take matters. Life is filled with dead-end streets, drop-offs, and dangerous terrain. You need a guide, and we are convinced that the guide you most desperately need is not one that tells you which career to choose, what city to live in, or who to marry. The orienteering aid you need is one that enables you to navigate your own heart.

The problem is, most of us can't define what the heart is, let alone explain how it works or where it is taking us. And make no mistake, your heart is taking you somewhere. Solomon, one of the wisest men who ever lived, wrote in Proverbs 4:23, "Above all else, guard your heart, for everything you do flows from it." Your heart is where the action is. Your heart is the launchpad for your life. Your heart is the one thing that impacts everything. So, you could say that having a reliable guide to how it works is incalculably important. But we don't want to just give you a guide to the heart. We want to guide you toward the kind of inside-out living that enables you to live focused, fulfilled, and fearless. We wrote this book so that you can live lionhearted.

PART 1

LET THE LION OUT

01

Most Wanted

Above all else, guard your heart, for
everything you do flows from it.

Proverbs 4:23

Every dude has a moment just like this locked within the
vault of his memory. It's dark. The house is still. Everyone
else is asleep, and you just heard a noise that you are 99.6
percent certain is a group of assassins, or at the very least
a crazed sociopath, who's breaking in to take your family out. This is not a drill. In a blurry-eyed panic, you
look around and realize that all you have to arm yourself
with is a bedside lamp from Target (you make a mental
note to move the baseball bat, currently in the garage, to
under your bed). But this is no time for woulda, coulda,
shoulda. It's time for you to defend the people you love.

You stealthily ease into the hallway because it's about to go down. Who are you? You are a preteen boy with a sharp sense of hearing and a healthy imagination.

If you grew up in the '90s, watching *America's Most Wanted* had you checking the locks on all your doors and windows before you went to bed at night. The present-day true crime podcast obsession was born out of host John Walsh ending each episode by reminding us, "You can make a difference." With these words, viewers across the United States were mobilized as amateur sleuths, and for two preteen boys (namely, David and Brandon Lindell), that call to action was simultaneously invigorating and horrifying.

Just think, desperate criminals could be all around you. They could be roaming your street or living in your neighborhood, and if you keep your eyes open, it could be your tip that leads to their arrest! On the other hand, *desperate criminals could be roaming your street and living in your neighborhood.* Terrifying.

Add to this that if we left our bedroom door open at night, we had a direct line of sight to our house's front door. Needless to say, we were on high alert.

The good news is the show frequently updated viewers on who had been arrested. Valiant citizens had watched the previous episodes, heeded the call, and tipped off the authorities. They had written down a vehicle description, recognized a face, or remembered a name, and now another bad guy was behind bars. Every time the show's host gave viewers information about who was now locked up, we breathed a subtle sigh of relief.

What you might not know is that *America's Most Wanted* was a personal passion project. John Walsh, the show's host, wasn't an actor, director, or television producer. He was a hotel executive and, more importantly, he was the dad of a six-year-old boy named Adam. On July 27, 1981, Adam was abducted from the toy aisle of a Florida department store. John never saw his son again, and out of that experience he not only cofounded the Center for Missing and Exploited Children, he also helped launch the show *America's Most Wanted*. Out of devasting personal tragedy, John's passion fueled the show through twenty-seven seasons and led to the capture of 1,200 suspects who were on the run because what John wanted most was to see perpetrators of violent crimes brought to justice.

This book is not a true crime anthology, but the origin story of *America's Most Wanted* does speak to the simple power of wanting to see something done. It is a poignant reminder of the power of making something your top priority. You may want a lot of things in life, but very likely it is what you want most that will actually get done.

Maybe you should stop right now and think about what is most important to you. For many men, this kind of introspective exercise is exactly what you don't want to do. But before you put this book down, labeling it self-help, touchy-feely garbage, we need to tell you something. God created you with the heart of a lion. He created you that way for a purpose, with the capacity to rule in life rather than being ruled by life. He created you with the amazing ability to decide and pursue what's most important.

It's for moments like this that you were created to decide whether you are going to stop medicating symptoms of a life you don't want and build the life you were created to live. To live lionhearted begins with asking yourself tough and pointed questions. So let us ask you: What do *you* want most out of life? What do you *want* most out of life?

A great career?
Financial independence?
A strong marriage?
Healthy, well-adjusted children?
An admired legacy?
A deep walk with God?

What should you prioritize?

Now, let us ask you this: What if there is one thing that changes everything? What if getting that right dramatically increases your ability to succeed in all those areas? How important would it be to get that one thing right?

Roughly three thousand years ago, a collection of sayings on the well-lived life was compiled by an ancient Near Eastern king named Solomon. Today you can find these sayings in the Old Testament book of Proverbs. Solomon presided over a golden era in the nation of Israel. During his reign, foreign dignitaries and royalty traveled not only to admire the splendor of Solomon's kingdom but also to learn from the wisdom he possessed. He is said to be one of the wisest people who ever lived. Solomon wrote about the hot topics of relationships, money, work, and sex. He also penned one incredibly powerful line that cuts straight to the center of what dictates everything else about your life. It's the one thing that changes everything.

Above all else, guard your heart, for everything you do flows from it. (Prov. 4:23)

In the most literal sense, it seems that Solomon is dispensing physiological insight that was way ahead of his time—heart disease is still the number one killer of men in the United States. Regardless of whether Solomon understood human anatomy, he wasn't talking about cardiovascular health, important as that is. He was talking about the interior life of a person.

When the Bible talks about the heart, it is referencing the core of who you are, your innermost self, the center of your character, the guiding compass of your convictions. The capacity of your heart extends far beyond your emotions or feelings. When you see the "heart" referenced in Scripture, it speaks to the place that frames the whole of human existence, for good or for bad. And yet, though Solomon was not pointing us to a biological reality, it is important to note that one of the fascinating realities of the human condition is that the physical often mirrors the spiritual, and the spiritual often mirrors the physical (more on that later). Just as heart health physically affects every other area of our body, so the health of our soul—what the Bible calls our "heart"—determines the health of every other part of our life.

Your physical heart is an engine pumping one hundred thousand times a day, sending blood down a sixty-thousand-mile-long vascular highway that runs throughout your body, and if your heart isn't working, you will know. There are all kinds of indicators: chest pain, fatigue, shortness of breath. The problem is, many times we are more attuned to our physiological realities than our spiritual realities. We get annual checkups. We count steps. We go to the gym. We take supplements and cut back on saturated fats. We pay attention to our bodies.

You can tell when your heart rate is off, but how do you know when your soul is off? What would tell you that something is sick at the core of who you are? Unfortunately, like with physical heart disease, if you aren't paying attention to subtle indicators, then over time symptoms give way to more dramatic consequences. Your wife is leaving you. You are fired for inappropriate behavior. You are drunk in front of your kids. You are considering leaving and ending it all. You may not be there today, but you are beginning to see signs pointing to major issues. And if you saw the signs and found out something was terribly wrong, what would you do about it? If the condition of your heart was affecting your family, your career, your relationships with people, your relationship with God, your faith, your strength, your dreams, and your future . . . would you know what to do?

Above All

In Proverbs 4:23, Solomon uses the Hebrew term *mikkol*, translated "above all," which signals that he is highlighting a comparison.[1] In other words, he is intentionally raising the question of what matters most to us, comparing the guarding of your heart to *everything* else. At some point, you must decide what you are going to pay attention to in life. You may have heard it said, "If everything is important, then nothing is important," and that's true. Every young dad knows this (and if you are not a dad, trust us on this one). We each have four kids. They are a built-in adventure. Sleep is the only respite from their unending quest to squeeze all the juice out of the lemon of life. Kids want to do everything all at once. And it's their insatiable appetite for anything fun that is literally one of the best parts of life.

Before those babies were born, our days were filled with margin. This is why it's hilarious to us when kidless college students opine about how busy they are. Becoming a parent has a way of putting time in perspective. Before, we could do anything we wanted at any time we wanted. But as a parent, you prioritize. Gone are the days of haphazard decision-making. It becomes about what you have to get done versus what you wanted to get done. Life with kids forces you to decide what is going to be most important. That's what Solomon is getting at when he uses the word *mikkol* (above all). You are going to have to make some "above all" decisions.

Ultimately, something will ALWAYS be prioritized above all else. You can choose it intentionally, or it can happen unintentionally. It's the latter that becomes true for most men. They never set out to become a workaholic. It just happened. They never intended to make life all about success and personal ambition. It just happened. They never meant to choose things that in the end won't matter. It just happened. There's a name for the it-just-happened way of living life. It's called *haphazard*. *Haphazard* is a combination of two words, the old English word *hap*, which means "happening" or "fortune," and *hazard*, which commonly refers to something dangerous, but in the past, it referred to a dice game based on chance, like craps. In other words, if you are living without making a clear decision about what is going to matter most, you have turned your whole existence into a roll of the dice. That's not going to make for a life well lived.

The Disease of Purposelessness

Rick Warren writes, "Henry David Thoreau observed that people live lives of 'quiet desperation,' but today a better description is aimless distraction," and sadly the sociological data bear that out.[2] Survey after survey suggests many men spend much of their time staring at screens, binge-watching Netflix, or playing video games. Oh, and they watch a lot of pornography too. In their article "How Prevalent is Pornography?," Daniel Cox, Beatrice Lee, and Dana Popky write, "Men in their 30s and 40s report the most frequent use of pornography. A majority (57 percent) of men ages 30–49 report having watched pornography in the past month, and 42 percent say they have watched it in the past week."[3] Also, as many as seven million men in their prime aren't working and instead are hanging out in front of a screen for an average of two thousand hours a year, which is approximately the time most people spend working a full-time job.[4] Additionally, according to the CDC, from 2001 to 2021, the suicide rate for men in the US was about four times as high as it was for women.[5] Men are facing a crisis of purposelessness. Richard Reeves, who wrote *Of Boys and Men*, bluntly states how bad the current situation has become: "Men are also much more likely to commit suicide than women. This is a worldwide, long-standing pattern. But the gender gap is widest in more advanced economies."[6] This startling reality illustrates the severity of this crisis facing modern men. Writing on masculinity, Barrett Swanson says, "Several of my male friends struggled with addiction and depression, or other conditions that could be named, but the more common complaint was something vaguer. . . . A quiet desperation that, if I were forced to generalize, seemed to stem from a gnawing sense of purposelessness."[7]

Many men live under this weight, and therefore they find it impossible to see the events of their lives or their decisions as having any inherent significance. And if your days don't ultimately matter, then it seems easier to just sleepwalk through life. But God didn't create you simply to exist. God didn't design you to endure. God didn't give you life and breath to punch a clock for fifty years just so you could live out the rest of your days waiting to die. You can stop looking at yourself as merely a cog in the machine of life, and instead see yourself as a lion. Your Creator is called the Lion of Judah, and you were created in His image. This means that you are a lot more lionlike than you may think or than you may be living.

The Life of a Lion

Everything about lions speaks of intentionality. They are the opposite of purposeless. Every move has a goal. Every sound has meaning. They know their territory—what's theirs to defend and protect. They are patient in their pursuits. Can the same be said about us?

The unintentional life is an aimless life, and what the writer of Proverbs is calling us to—what God is calling us to—is nothing less than a radical reprioritizing of what we care about. Now, it's possible the thought of being intentional sounds exhausting. This might be because currently the only similarity between you and an actual lion is the fact that lions can nap twenty-three hours a day. But don't be discouraged. This is not a journey you will accomplish in a day or a road you will travel alone. The Lion of the tribe of Judah, the God-man, Jesus Christ, will help you. He is not going to spoon-feed you and coddle your weakness, but He will help you in your weakness with His strength.

Jesus was the one who said, "From the heart come evil thoughts, murder, adultery, all sexual immorality, theft, lying, and slander."[8] The deprioritized and dysfunctional heart can introduce an unimaginable level of brokenness into your life. Deciding to do a hard reset on what you value above all else is going to require a radical shift. But until you decide to make the core of who you are the "above all" issue of your life, nothing else gets better. The journey of purpose and intentionality begins by connecting with who God has created you to be, one decision at a time. The first step is knowing what is happening right now in the deepest part of you—your heart. You can have the heart of a lion; you may just need the Lion to reveal it to you.

Something Needs to Change

John Maxwell notes that there are three reasons why people change: "People change when they . . . Hurt enough that they have to, Learn enough that they want to, and Receive enough that they are able to."[9] You are very likely reading this book because on some level you know there are things in your life that need to change. Maybe you've recognized things are off, but you haven't been able to put your finger on what's really going on. Or maybe you have fought off a gnawing sense of purposelessness and restless angst for far too long.

For most of us it is pain that becomes the catalyst to change. You might see troubling signs in your family life. You and your spouse are constantly at each other, and the relationship just seems to be getting worse. It feels like your kids are slipping away. Your thoughts are a toxic, dystopian wasteland. You recognize there is a massive disconnect between who people think you are and who you really are. Maybe you are sick and tired of being sick and tired.

It could be that you have attempted to make surface-level life changes that simply didn't work. You started another year with resolutions and new habits, but you have once again been disappointed to find that you are still you. Nothing has ultimately changed. Experience has taught you enough to know that something deeper is happening and something deeper is needed to become who you want to be.

Something needs to happen to position us to live the life we want to live and propel us into the future we desire. You have to receive what enables you to change. You CANNOT change, and your life WILL NOT change until you accept the simple truth that everything you are dreaming for your life starts with the core of who you are. Starting anywhere else is like tinkering with a broken clock.

You can make adjustments, but ultimately it's still off. That's what this book is about. It's a reset on the inside. It's a deep dive into what makes you tick. It's looking at your life from the foundational acknowledgment that God wired you to live life from the heart, and until that is right, nothing will be.

So, where do we go from here? It's time to prioritize the one thing that changes everything. It's time to set your sights on fighting for your future. It's time to begin living from the inside out.

02

Hell in Your Heart

The heart is deceitful above all things, and
desperately wicked; who can know it?
Jeremiah 17:9 NKJV

The heart of man is his worst part.
John Flavel

The footage is dimly lit and eerie. A tinge of sweat on
his brow, a man points to his wristwatch and says, in a
nervous but determined voice, "Look, this is for you. It's
not a watch. It's a detonator to kill as much as I can, God
willing. But this is meant to kill you. . . . You will be sent
to [hell]." These were some of the last known words of
Dr. Humam al-Balawi before his suicide mission.

The bomb exploded just five days after Christmas. Lethal shrapnel—a cocktail of ball bearings, broken glass, and even children's toy metal jacks—shot nearly fifty feet in every direction, easily slicing through human flesh. The explosion killed six people instantly. Four more lives were lost in the hours that followed as people succumbed to the horrific injuries they had sustained from the blast.

The scene of this tragedy was not a battlefield but the center of a military base—a place that was supposed to be secure. The attack did not come from the outside but from the inside. This explosion was not caused by a missile, an IED, or a coordinated military offensive. This assault had a more sinister source. It was a mole.

Dr. al-Balawi had fooled the top spy organization in the world. This triple agent had successfully gained the trust of the Central Intelligence Agency and through his deception caused one of the deadliest events in CIA history.

Before al-Balawi became an informant for the US military, he was a medical doctor living a quiet life in Jordan. With no known military history, he volunteered to aid the United States by infiltrating terrorist networks.

At the time, the hunt for Osama bin Laden, the mastermind of the September 11 attacks, was in full swing. The pressure and potential prestige of finding public enemy number one blinded CIA personnel to the numerous red flags al-Balawi presented. Unfortunately, these warning signs only became obvious with the benefit of hindsight, when it was too late.

Shockingly, on the day of the bombing, al-Balawi had less security scrutiny than any other individual admitted to the base. The lore and excitement that surrounded this prized informant made missing his true identity as a deadly terrorist all too easy. They didn't even notice the thirty-pound vest loaded with C4 strapped to his chest. With a watch that doubled as a detonator, this deceptive suicide bomber moved easily to a location for maximum casualties. After making a short speech, he yelled "Allahu Akbar" and hit the button.[1]

Warnings were ignored, distraction prevailed, priorities were misplaced, and hell was ushered straight into the heart of a military base. Then–CIA director Leon Panetta said, "Missteps occurred because of shortcomings across several agency components in areas including communications, documentation and management oversight."[2] Or as author Joby Warrick more bluntly puts it, "No one really saw this coming."[3] Everyone was focused on the threats that existed outside the walls of the compound, but the greatest vulnerability was on the inside.

You might be thinking, "Wow, what a cheerful beginning to this chapter. Thank you for depressing me." In our defense, you ARE reading a chapter titled "Hell in Your Heart." Depression is not our aim, but an emotional reaction, a check in your thought processes, or even shock is. Why? Because it is very possible you are being deceived. You need to wake up! You need to stop blaming everything and everyone except yourself as the source of the problem. This is critical before we move forward. You must understand it is not only possible but very likely you are dealing with a mole in your soul, an internal double agent, and this shrapnel-spraying, C4-carrying terrorist is in YOU. The best thing you can do is let that sink in and face the facts.

It's easy to assume the most damaging attacks against you will come from the outside. It's easy to assume that the danger comes from broken trust, a deal gone wrong, a relationship that soured, or even from Satan himself. But the greatest area of weakness for any man resides at the center of who he is.

Your heart will rob you.

Your heart will deceive you.

Your heart will condemn you.

Your heart will expose you to the enemy.

Seventeenth-century British pastor, author, and theologian John Flavel writes, "The heart of man is his worst part before it is regenerated."[4] Jesus is even more graphic in his negative portrayal of the heart. He says, "For from within, out of the heart of man, come evil thoughts, sexual immorality, theft, murder, adultery."[5] The description cannot get more dire than that.

Yet, the problem is we live in a world that is totally oblivious to this reality. We hear a constant refrain of "listen to your heart," "follow your heart," "be true to yourself." But what if the heart you are listening to and the self you are being true to is actively working against you and everything you were created to become?

"Follow Your Heart" Is Terrible Advice

We live in a culture that continually calls men to base their direction and their decisions on pseudo-wisdom that would be best suited for a fortune cookie. The cliché "follow your heart" is a perfect example. It's terrible advice that our society has gobbled up like ice cream.

It sounds harmless, but it's an invitation to unleash hell. The call to follow your heart is essentially a euphemism to "do what you feel," and by any metric, that approach to life is failing men miserably. With most young adult American males now giving hours every day to gaming, binge-watching, and consuming porn, suicide rates have risen rapidly, and drug use among young men has skyrocketed.[6]

Let's just think about the impact of porn for a minute. One study noted that just between 2004 and 2016, porn use rose 310 percent, with young men ages eighteen to twenty-five being the primary consumers of explicit content.[7] In 2022, Pornhub logged over 2.14 billion site visits in a single month, surpassing the total web traffic to Instagram, Netflix, Pinterest, and TikTok combined.[8] Added to that, men are more likely than ever to avoid the responsibility that comes with marriage and children. They are choosing to stay single longer and cohabitate instead of marrying. This in turn has produced the shocking reality that in a study of 130 countries and territories, American children rank as the most likely to grow up in single-parent homes.[9] Yet, not only is this "porndemic" creating massive problems for families and children, it's also killing men's sexual satisfaction—leading to loneliness and insecurity.[10]

This deadly concoction of pleasure, leisure, and laziness calls out to young men on every street corner. And as Neil Postman writes, "When cultural life is redefined as a perpetual round of entertainments . . . then a nation finds itself at risk; culture-death is a clear possibility."[11] Generations of young men following their hearts and living for the moment has produced a hellish reality for them and for the people who depend on them. As our good friend Josh Hawley notes, "No menace to this nation is greater than the collapse of American manhood."[12]

Just looking at the world forces you to admit something is terribly wrong and only seems to be getting worse. And yet the temptation is to blame external forces.

It's the government!
It's corruption!
It's liberalism!
It's the media!
It's Hollywood!
It's . . . !

The problem is that God doesn't lay the blame in those places. Scripture is clear that what's killing you is not an assault from the outside but decay on the inside. So there is a sense in which the atheistic German philosopher Friedrich Nietzsche was right on target when he wrote, "But the worst enemy you can meet, will you yourself always be; you waylay yourself in caverns and forests. You lonesome one, you go the way to yourself! And past yourself and your seven devils leads your way! A heretic will you be to yourself, and a wizard and a soothsayer, and a fool, and a doubter, and a reprobate, and a villain."[13] On this point, Nietzsche finds himself in agreement with what the Bible says about what's going on at the core of who you are. Now, before you take this book and shove it down the garbage disposal, thinking, "I don't need this negative nonsense," take a moment to ask yourself some questions:

Could this be true of me?

Could hell be in my heart?

If your reaction to either question is a sort of tough-guy denial, the "Heck no, I'm good" approach, then we suggest giving this book to a friend and rebuying it when you are ready for the real talk that comes with honest self-examination, which will actually bring lasting change to your life.

That's why you picked up this book, isn't it? You need this. Most guys don't read a book like this because they are nailing it. They grab a book like this because they know everything is not quite right on the inside. Our guess is that you are keenly aware of that reality as well. You made it to chapter two because you realize things are not going as well as you would want them to—or at least as good as everyone around you might think. You are fighting hidden battles. You are facing internal struggles. You are carrying broken promises. You are wrestling with relational trauma. You are angry. You want to quit. And the list goes on. There are areas of your life where you are saying, "I am losing, but I want to win." So, let us ask you again: Could there be some hell in your heart? Could that rot that sin introduced into the world be eating away at your soul? As the theologian John Owen writes, "Be killing sin or sin will be killing you."[14] That's what hell in your heart does.

While that's a difficult thing to admit, it is the first step on the path to becoming lionhearted. If the CIA had asked more hard questions rather than operating out of blissful naivete, things would have been different. Inquiries would have been made. Difficult conversations would have been had. Mistakes would have been corrected. Changes would have been put into effect. And ultimately lives would have been saved.

When al-Balawi moved to Pakistan as an unknown, he had no experience in espionage, yet he very quickly was able to connect with high-ranking US counterterrorism personnel. He even sent a video back to the CIA showing himself in a meeting with leaders of an anti-American terror group. This immediately shot excitement through the intelligence agency because they had been lacking quality leads for so long. It was just the sugary coating they needed to be self-deceived. He gave them information about drone targets that sacrificed people to ensure that further credibility was established. At that point, desire and self-deception stopped critical questions from being asked.

No one looked deeper into his past.

No one asked how it was possible for him to film that video if he was unknown.

No one thought to search him before he stepped onto an American base.

And hellish results were realized.

From our vantage point, we could say, "Well, they were idiots." Not so fast. Is it possible you are doing the same thing? Going about your business, whistling happily as you step in front of the bus of hell that rules the highways of your heart? That is exactly what you are doing when you say things like, "The problem isn't me," "I don't need help," "I am fine," "I am just being me." It is the same as letting a terrorist into the core of who you are and saying, "No search necessary."

Instead, if you dare to do a vital, albeit painful, exercise of discovering what is really happening at the core of who you are, then the best question to start with is: How did hell make it inside my heart in the first place? To answer that question, we have to go all the way back to the beginning, the very beginning.

A Holy Take on Your Hellish Heart

The first humans who ever walked the planet were Adam and Eve. Scripture tells us that God described everything about their original existence as "very good."[15] They were enjoying their relationship with God. They were enjoying the fulfillment of their purpose. They lived naked and unashamed, so it's safe to say they were enjoying each other as well! And yet, in the midst of all this goodness, Satan began to whisper that God was holding out on them. There was only one "thou shalt not" in the entire world for them, and that was that they weren't supposed eat from the tree of the knowledge of good and evil.

> The LORD God warned him, "You may freely eat the fruit of every tree in the garden—except the tree of the knowledge of good and evil. If you eat its fruit, you are sure to die."[16]

This one command is where Satan centered his attack.

> "You won't die!" the serpent replied to the woman. "God knows that your eyes will be opened as soon as you eat it, and you will be like God, knowing both good and evil."[17]

He told them that God was bluffing and that He was insecure about them knowing as much as He did. And they bought it. They ate the fruit and, in that act, perpetuated cosmic treason against their Creator and closest friend.

What our first parents didn't realize is that part of the *death* that God had warned them about was the unleashing of hell in the heart of every person in the human race. This universal internal brokenness is something theologians refer to as total depravity. R. C. Sproul puts our situation bluntly when he says, "Our minds have been darkened by sin and our desires bound by the wicked impulses. But we can still think, choose, and act. Yet something terrible has happened to us. We have lost all desire for God. The thoughts and desires of our heart are only evil continuously."[18] The hellishness of sin affects and infects every facet of who we are, especially our hearts.

One of the most well-written statements articulating the reality every human being is born into are the words of the Old Testament prophet Jeremiah: "The heart is deceitful above all things, and desperately wicked; who can know it?"[19]

Here is a thought: God, the Creator of the human soul, says that what will deceive you "above all things" is in YOU. But here's the crazy part. Jeremiah not only says the heart is deceitful and wicked, he then adds that nobody can understand what is really going on in their heart. The inevitable conclusion? If you feel good about the "reasons" you can articulate for WHY you do what you do, maybe you shouldn't. The enemy of our existence—who is completely against you being a strong, healthy, whole, God-honoring, hell-storming man—pretends to be an angel of light. Why is that relevant? It's important to note because he is an expert in co-opting the sinful disposition of the human heart to carry out his own plans through people. He will use the self-deceiving tendency of your heart to his advantage and to your destruction. Erwin Lutzer echoes this truth about Satan: "His strategy is to give people what they want but to make sure they eventually get what he wants them to have."[20] Spoiler alert: What he wants you to have is hell as your permanent residence. He will tell you that the lie you tell yourself is actually wisdom, and then he will work overtime to replay the soundtrack of his sinful narrative over and over in your heart. What does it sound like?

Like refrains you have probably heard before:

Watching porn is relieving stress and helping my marriage.

Fantasizing about that person is a harmless diversion.

Cheating is about personal happiness since my spouse isn't meeting my needs.

Leaving is right because I need to make a personal health decision to get space.

As long as it doesn't hurt anyone else, then it can't be wrong.

I can handle this.

God wants me to be happy.

Notice how each one of those sentences sounds positive. They include words like *helping*, *happiness*, and *health*. On the surface, they sound wise, but they are all part of a "wisdom" that is straight from hell and headed back to hell. The New Testament writer James says there is a brand of "wisdom" that gets a lot of airtime in the world that at its core is "earthly, unspiritual, demonic."[21] Notice that the refrains above center on self-gratification—a hallmark of the demonic "wisdom" James talks about is also an "all-about-me attitude" that often reveals itself through envy and selfish ambition. James is pointing us to the reality that this hellish pseudo-wisdom goes all the way back to Genesis 3, where Adam and Eve bought into the demonic lie that doing things that looked, felt, and seemed right to them would be better than doing things God's way.[22] That's why "following your heart" is a train wreck way to live your life.

But, for argument's sake, let's say you are trying to do the right thing. You want to be a good man. You want to be a good husband, a good father, a good employee, a good citizen. Maybe you would even go so far as to say you want to be a godly man. And you're making serious efforts in these areas. The major problem with trying to live out your God-given purpose with a heart that is bent toward darkness and dysfunction is that your efforts will ultimately lead to frustration—which is exactly why the apostle Paul, one of the most well-known characters in the whole Bible, says, "I have discovered this principle of life—that when I want to do what is right, I inevitably do what is wrong."[23] The fact of the matter is that you will never get life right with a wrong heart because the core of who you are is fundamentally oriented in the wrong direction.

The two of us have an ongoing brotherly debate about camping. One of us loves to hike into the wilderness with only what can be carried on his back, and the other one not so much. But both of us agree that it's almost impossible to have fun roughing it out in the wild without the right equipment. If you don't have the right gear, a weekend off the grid can get miserable in a hurry, and one of the essentials you need if you are going to venture out in the unknown is a compass. And yet not every compass is created equal. Our kids have had compasses that wouldn't help you find your way out of a wet paper bag, let alone the backside of a national park. The needles no longer tell the truth about which direction you are headed (oh, the joys of dollar store camping equipment). It's fine, as long as you don't use it to determine your course. The fact is, no one consciously chooses to go to hell or even to be the kind of person who belongs in hell, it's just that their internal compass (i.e., their heart) won't let them go anywhere else. Most people aren't trying to make hell at home in their heart, it just seems to be the way things naturally go. Jeremiah shows us the reason is that the heart's needle only points toward hell until something dramatic shifts at the center of your life—a shift that empowers you to live lionhearted.[24] That shift is what the rest of this book is about.

03

Getting the Hell Out
of Your Heart

The heart of man is his worst part before it
is regenerated, and the best afterwards.

John Flavel

I will give you a new heart and put a new spirit
in you; I will remove from you your heart
of stone and give you a heart of flesh.

Ezekiel 36:26

Coke or Pepsi? A loaded question, to be sure. Statistics say
most of you (in your head) just answered, "Coke, duh."
So, let us introduce . . . "The Pepsi Paradox."

The surprising truth is that while most people say they prefer Coke to Pepsi, throughout the past century, thousands of blind taste tests have verified that people overwhelmingly prefer Pepsi's flavor. What? How? Crazy as it sounds, Coke is well aware of this phenomenon. So, you may be wondering, "If Coke knows, why wouldn't they just tweak their formula slightly and crush Pepsi once and for all?" Great question. The answer is, they tried, and it was an unmitigated disaster.[1]

Have you ever heard of New Coke? We didn't think so. Let us set the stage for you. The year was 1985. Pepsi came up with a brilliant marketing campaign known as the "Pepsi challenge." They performed blind taste tests on camera, and as you now know, people overwhelmingly picked Pepsi instead of Coke. Pepsi started to gain market share. In fact, the ads were so successful that Coke executives began to worry and felt they had to do something. So they came up with a new formula and named it New Coke (we would have loved to have been in this pitch meeting!). When New Coke was launched, they were so committed to this new recipe that they locked the original Coke formula in a vault in Atlanta, deciding it would never see the light of day again. Coke's chief executive officer, Roberto Goizueta, said, "Some may choose to call this the boldest single marketing move in the history of the packaged-goods business. We simply call it the surest move ever made." Coca-Cola's president Donald Keough said, "I've never been as confident about a decision as I am about the one we're announcing today." His poor wife . . . we hope that guy wasn't married. New Coke turned out to be a disaster. Their confidence was met with thousands of angry phone calls, which peaked at eight thousand un-comfortable conversations per day. Finally, a decision was made to abruptly change course.[2]

A mere seventy-nine days after their initial announce-ment, another press conference was held, reversing their decision by returning to the original formula, now called Coca-Cola Classic. Before we say, "Yep, those guys are idi-ots" or "I would have never done that," you should know they made the decision based on what they thought was solid data. They performed their own blind taste test with 190,000 people, proving to even Coke's top-tier executives that the majority of the consumers preferred Pepsi. The issue was they were trying to solve their problem in the completely wrong way. Mind-blowing!

This story presents us with a stark truth. You can think you "know" what to do based on what you see and still be dead wrong. You could be coming up with solutions that look great on paper but take you to disaster because there is more than meets the eye. If this is true for soft drink marketing, how much more for the human heart? When you study Scripture, you find this truth at work: spiritual realities are the greater realities. Hopefully a light bulb is turning on for you as you come to the realization that your overconfident solutions to fix your personal life are underproducing. The ultimate bummer is when you are working hard to do something that isn't working at all; when you are putting in tons of effort and resources only to fail because the core is wrong. In today's dollars, Coke spent nearly $100 million dollars to make a change that left them with nothing to show for it. As the saying goes, they missed the forest for the trees—they missed the point.

Your mind, soul, and spirit are so conspicuously mundane, so familiar, that when problems arise, you can easily find yourself believing that you can fix you. You can commit to a new routine. Set goals. Take vitamins. Stay positive. Be nice. Give to charity. Phrases like, "I got myself into this so I can get myself out" or "I'll just get through it" might be a regular part of your internal narrative. This kind of thinking is like drywalling over a leaky pipe and calling it good: a recipe for disaster. You need to see your heart as something you can manage but not repair. Think about the fencing surrounding an electrical plant: "Danger! High Voltage. Keep Out!" When you see a sign like that, it doesn't mean no one can go in. It means only those with the right knowledge, expertise, and safety equipment should go in. If you try to fix your heart on your own, you will end up like the stick figure on the sign being struck by a lightning bolt. The heart is a complex, high-voltage creation of the most-high God. The heart resides at the center of your being, the center of the masterpiece God crafted that is you.

Defaced but Not Erased

When you look at your internal world, *masterpiece* might not be the word that comes to mind, but don't look at who you are now. Think design, think who you were intended to be: lionhearted. If you think about that too long, the gap between your current state and that idea might seem so far apart that you want to give up. Perfect. That's what you need to do—give up. Quit. Adios. Stop trying. You can't fix your internal world. You can't change your heart. Someone needs to tell you that because you have been lied to. You have been indoctrinated by millions of signs, movies, songs, and advertisements that celebrate your self-reliance. So, when you hear us say you can't fix your own heart, you probably don't believe it and consequently you are stuck—or worse, dying inside. So, we are kindly going to yell at you in writing: YOU CAN'T FIX YOURSELF!!! Maybe you should say it out loud right now: "I CAN'T FIX MYSELF."

The truth will set you free! Don't you feel better?

Recently we came across an article about a painting from the British royal family's collection that dates back to the seventeenth century. Over the course of centuries, this masterpiece had been covered by paint, stains, and other foreign chemicals until you couldn't even see the original creation anymore. It had to be painstakingly restored, millimeter by millimeter, by a master restorationist to make the original artwork visible. That's what you need. God made you in His image (what theologians refer to as the *imago Dei*); however, you may look at your life and not see even the faintest hint of the Creator you were made to reflect. All you may be able to see is built-up brokenness that sin has left in its wake. But no matter how marred the canvas of your life may be, the original design is still there, defaced but not erased. The *imago Dei* still lingers under the surface, and yet the damage is so great that this isn't a restoration job you are capable of undertaking on your own. It calls for the Master who created the masterpiece to do something at the center of you that you could never do for yourself.

Heart Transplant

If he didn't agree to the operation he would die. That sounds like an easy decision, except for the fact that the procedure in question had never been attempted. The year was 1967, and Louis Washkansky desperately needed a full heart transplant. The problem was that the only successful operation of this kind that had ever been performed had been on a dog.

Eight years earlier in 1959, Dr. Norman Shumway, nicknamed the "the king of hearts" (true story), had transplanted a heart from one dog to another. The good news is that the dog survived the surgery. The bad news is that it only lived for eight days.[3]

Now the question was, would Louis agree to undergo a procedure that had never successfully been performed on a grown man? The reality is he had no choice. He desperately needed a new heart.

The same is true for every man reading this book. A heart transplant is your only option because, as we have already established, you can't fix you. That's not to say that people don't try. It just never works.

We should probably stop for a second and acknowledge that this whole idea of you needing to be fixed is a countercultural idea, and an enormously unpopular one. "The Most Quoted Man Alive," Steve Maraboli, has famously said, "Stop trying to 'fix' yourself; you're not broken!"[4] We don't know Steve, but we do know he's not the only one giving voice to the notion that there is nothing wrong with humanity. The problem is that no intellectually honest assessment of the status quo or the historical trajectory of humankind would validate this widely embraced brand of pop psychology. There's just too much brokenness on Planet Earth that we would have to willfully ignore to maintain this fiction.

And yet, human beings love to revel in the fantasy of their own self-determination, self-improvement, self-confidence, self-empowerment, self-transformation, and even self-mastery. The anthem of self, self, self, self is in the air we breathe. We love to talk about the self-made and the self-reliant. The problem? There is no such thing.

We are not saying self-improvement isn't possible or valuable. You can get better. You can grow. You can improve. In fact, it's essential to becoming all that God created you to be, and we are going to unpack how this happens in the chapters ahead. But the launching pad for any growth and improvement that actually counts in life is the work God alone can do in you. You may have heard it said, "God loves you just the way you are, but He doesn't want you to stay that way." And the good news is it's what He does in your life that frees you from staying stuck where you are.

Trying to remedy what's fundamentally broken at the center of every person (including you) is the problem that stands in the way of you experiencing any deep and lasting change and requires a supernatural solution. That's not our opinion, that's the repeated contention of the writers of Scripture and the continual reframing of Christian theologians for the last two thousand years. The good news is that God is better acquainted with the desperate nature of your situation than you ever could be, and He makes a promise in the pages of the Old Testament through the pen of a prophet named Ezekiel.

I will give you a new heart and put a new spirit in you; I will remove from you your heart of stone and give you a heart of flesh.[5]

These words articulate a dynamic contrast: your old heart vs. your new heart. Your old heart (for many, your current heart) is as dead, cold, lifeless, and hard as a rock. The center of who you are is ultimately stubborn and unresponsive to God. That's why your condition necessitates a transplant.

You can't get better until God does surgery at the center of who you are. That is not to say you cannot have "spiritual" experiences or feel God's presence or even make moral choices—it's just that none of those things will effect true and lasting transformation in your life as long as you are living with a cold, dead heart. In fact, one of the scariest realities about the human heart is that exposure to God's presence, God's voice, and God's Word can actually make it worse. This is the chilling warning tucked away in the book of Hebrews that should cause your hair to stand on end if you are seeking spiritual experiences without genuine relationship with Jesus: "The Holy Spirit says, 'Today when you hear his voice, don't harden your hearts.'"[6] You cannot fix your hard heart, but you can make it harder.

Every time a person hears God calling them but doesn't respond, they make it that much more difficult to respond the next time God speaks. Some of you know exactly what we are talking about. You used to hear God, but those days are long gone. You used to be more interested and open, but that has now been replaced with apathy. You used to feel the desire, but that has been displaced by deadness. Your heart is getting harder and harder. Hell is more entrenched than ever before, and as burly nineteenth-century English preacher Charles Spurgeon (who you are going bump into in these pages again and again) puts it, "A man who has a hard heart is Satan's throne."[7] Why would he say that? Because when your heart is hard to God's voice, what Satan says goes. That sounds extreme, but it's true. Not only does your internal hardness make you less prepared to receive God's Word, but it is also readier to reject God's way. The callousness at the core of your life progressively silences your conscience along with the conviction of the Holy Spirit. You become comfortable with what used to trouble you. Where temptation once felt like a confrontation between good and evil, it now feels more like an invitation to do what you already know you want to do. Hardness fills your heart with darkness and suffocates light—this is the default of the human condition.

This sad state is precisely why the writer of Hebrews says, "Today when you hear his voice," because now is always the best time to ask God to deal with the deadness of your heart. Of course, this is most pressing for those who have not responded to the life-and-death message of salvation available in Jesus, but the startling reality is that hardness can creep back into your life even after you've started following Jesus. After all, the book of Hebrews was written to Christians. The warnings in Hebrews 3 are aimed at followers of Jesus, and the writer of Hebrews was quoting Psalm 95. Jews who read these verses knew this all instinctively. These words were the call to worship every Sabbath in the synagogue.[8] Their worship started with a gut check: Today you are going to encounter God's voice—are you ready? Are you prepared to listen? Are you willing to change? You get to choose how you are going to respond. You see, until you surrender your life to Jesus, there is no choice, only hardness. But with your new heart, there is a decision.

Time to Get Violent

When you become a Christian, you don't turn into a robot. You don't automatically choose life. You don't automatically choose purity. You don't automatically do the right thing. You don't automatically choose to line your life up with God's truth. But your new heart, empowered by the Holy Spirit, gives you the *ability* to choose.

Every time you encounter God's Word, you decide to either move toward God or dig in your heels. There is no such thing as neutrality in the life of faith. Jesus said, "The kingdom of heaven has suffered violence, and the violent take it by force."[9] When He said this, Jesus was acknowledging both the reality of demonic opposition along with the resolve necessary to experience the fullness of the kingdom of God in your life. It takes tenacity. It takes dogged determination. Passivity is not an option. God is always calling us closer to Him. What's your response? If you don't act when you hear His voice, you are making a choice to harden your heart. Inactivity is a vote to go back to living and looking like the old you. You are identifying more with the default of who you used to be before God transformed you than with the transformed you.

It's the easiest thing in the world for a Christian man to be too passive, and hardness sets in as a result. This hardness can even be brought on by things we would call good and godly. Going to church is a dangerous hobby. You are operating on the mistaken assumption that putting yourself in proximity to truth will be enough to provoke positive incremental change in you. Your spiritual outlook is the equivalent of the college student sleeping with a textbook under his pillow, hoping he can prepare for the exam by osmosis. The problem is that hearing God's Word without taking the dramatic action that it demands is doing damage to your soul. This is why so many Christian high school students head off to university only to come home as indifferent agnostics. They never learned that faith is a fight. They grew up with a religious label attached to their family's affiliation, but they never personally owned and went to war for their faith in Jesus.

If you are doing "spiritual" things—whether that's occasionally attending church, sporadically reading the Bible, or periodically listening to worship music—simply because that's what you do, that's the way you grew up, or you know that's what a Christian is supposed to do, you are playing games with life-and-death truth. Your docile disposition is killing the potential work of God in you. And what's so dangerous about that way of living is that the longer you allow that to continue unchecked, the more difficult it becomes to break the cycle. Passivity perpetuates passivity. You don't get to pick and choose when you are going to hear God's voice and obey His Word. You have to decide what will be the pattern in your life.

Maybe it's time to stop just going to church. Yes, you read that right, it's time to stop *just going* to church. What if you reframed your thinking about your walk with God?

What if you came to church with a "take it by force" mentality? What if you decided that for far too long you have been content with a brand of Christianity that's got the trappings and the lingo of Jesus but lacks the bare-knuckle desperation to do damage to darkness, and you opened your Bible to read from *that* mindset? This can be true of any place in our life where God is calling us to live like a lion, but we are being passive. Stop just being married. Stop just being a father. Stop just working your job. Stop just saying "I am what I am." Getting violent doesn't mean being hostile to those around you; it means being aggressive in taking personal responsibility for what is happening inside you and around you. Recognizing the new heart means you have power to change things. It's time for you to live like the stakes are high, because they are.

If God has given you a new heart, the choice is up you. You have been empowered to live the lionhearted life that not only has the authority to kick any vestiges of hell out of your own heart, but to drive back darkness wherever you find yourself. If that hasn't happened to you, it doesn't mean you are not trying to be a good person or even attempting to follow God. It does mean that you haven't experienced what only God can do in your life—in other words, what you can't do for yourself.

Maybe the best way to explain why you can't do this for yourself is to tell you a story. Years ago, we were grabbing dinner with Levi Lusko when he stopped the conversation and said, "I am very worried you are either going to burn your house to the ground or get yourself electrocuted." Levi's concern was palpable, and his worry wasn't unwarranted. Brandon was hilariously telling the story of a recent DIY misadventure, illustrating the danger of the project with his freshly bandaged hand. While we have the utmost respect for all the DIY aficionados reading this chapter, the unfortunate truth is we don't count ourselves among your ranks. Our DIY acronym would be better suited to mean "destroy it yourself."

Our enthusiasm and desire are always fueling optimism for the launch of each new project; however, we lack the essential ingredient of knowledge—a gap that we unsuccessfully try to fill with YouTube. So, there we sat at dinner, nervously laughing, listening to Brandon talk about how he changed fifteen outlets and a light switch in record time with no electrical experience only to cut open his hand and find the receptacles didn't work when he was done . . . sad.

Don't judge.

The issue was not actually a lack of knowledge. Videos were watched and instructions were followed. It's just that we all have areas of our life where DIY is not the best solution. You are simply not up to the task.

True, it may seem like handling a sagging deck or repairing a gas line yourself would be more convenient and cost-effective, but it can quickly go wrong, be extremely frustrating, and even be dangerous. If we had the time and inclination, we could solicit stories from every guy reading this book about some DIY project that started with so much promise only to cause you loads of irritation. This same principle is applicable beyond the realm of home projects; in fact, it is scarily poignant in relationship to your heart. As John Piper says, "If we are going to escape the hardness and deadness of that heart, the old heart has to be taken out, a new heart has to be put in—and we can't do that surgery on ourselves."[10] The beginning of living a lionhearted life that's full of all that God desires to do in you and through you starts with the new heart He alone can give you.

Some of you know this because you have experienced it. You remember the old you, and that's not who you are anymore. You know that the new you started with your new heart. For others reading this book, God brought you all the way to this page, because you know you need what only He can do. You need Him to do the lifesaving, eternity-altering, heaven-instead-of-hell, death-defeating operation that will make you brand new from the inside out. That's the gospel: that God in Christ by the power of the Holy Spirit does for us what we could never do for ourselves. The moment you ask God to save you, He re-creates your interior life by giving you a heart that is not only ready and able to respond to Him but is capable of being empowered to become the engine for lionhearted living. In that moment, God enforces an eviction notice for the hell in your heart, and gifts you a new heart to help you fulfill your purpose and calling.

But your new heart is just the beginning. Once God has done what only He can do on the inside, it makes way for everything He wants to do in you and through you to change the world around you. It could be that you have never experienced God giving you a new heart. You can be changed right now as you read this book by asking Jesus to give you a new heart and making Him the leader and King of your life. If you are a Christian but inside you are full of darkness, bitterness, and destructive thoughts, then rededicate your heart to Jesus. Just pray, "Jesus, I need You to give me a new heart. Please forgive me for how I have wronged You and others. I ask that You be the leader of my life. I give my life to You. Amen!" As you prayed that, it was a holy moment. God heard you. His presence is with you right now. You are going to see His power work miracles in your life. It doesn't mean it will be easy. He is not making you into a passive pussycat. He is making you into a lionhearted man. Be encouraged—you are on your way!

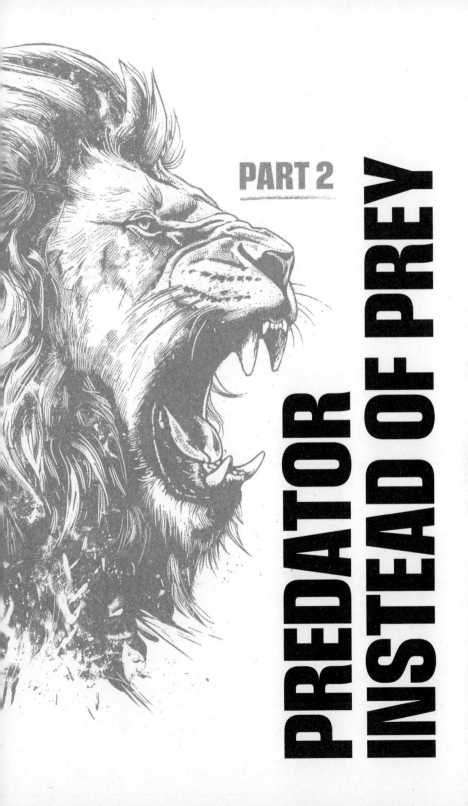

PART 2

PREDATOR
INSTEAD OF PREY

04

The Inner Life of a Lion

Therefore, if anyone is in Christ, the new creation
has come: The old has gone, the new is here!

2 Corinthians 5:17

The deepest sense of "heart" is the
genuine, the authentic man.

F. H. von Meyenfeldt

The engine made all the difference for King Richard. Not
the twelfth-century English monarch, Richard the Lionhearted, but Richard "The King" Petty. This cowboy
hat–wearing NASCAR driver, famous for his shades and
his stache, is one of the most celebrated and respected

racers in motorsports history. However, this titan of the NASCAR world was not always known as "The King."

Richard's father, Lee Petty, also an accomplished driver, won the inaugural race at the Daytona Speedway when Richard was twenty-one and just beginning his own racing career. Both Lee and Richard had a knack for showmanship and had highly competitive personalities. So "driven" (pun intended) was the Petty family that when Richard defeated his father in the 1959 Lakewood 500 race, Lee protested his own son's victory, arguing Richard was unfairly given an extra lap. Lee was ultimately correct, and Richard's win was overturned. While this could have been a bit of an awkward family situation, they both were good sports about it.[1]

Not one to get discouraged, Richard's big break would come five years later when he raced in the Daytona 500 at twenty-six years old. Spoiler alert: He would win and win big. In this race, he led 184 of the 200 laps, setting a Daytona 500 record that has never been matched. This launched Richard Petty into a new level of fame, complete with a new name: "The King."

How did this happen? It wasn't his racing pedigree, personal effort, or an amazing team around him. It was a brand-new type of engine. When Richard sat behind the wheel in February 1964, he was driving a car with a state-of-the-art Chrysler 426 Hemi engine. The 426 was specifically developed for this race and would make Hemis so well-known that they are still popular to this day. Hemi (short for hemispherical) engines had been around since 1905, when a Belgian automaker named Pipe dropped one into a 130hp Fiat Grand Prix race car. The 426 Richard

Petty captained was an absolute monster, light-years ahead of the Fiat and engineered to perfection . . . well, almost.

Less than a month prior to the race, Chrysler discovered imperfections in the engine block. The 426 Hemi would not stand up to the stress of the Daytona 500 unless this was fixed and fast. With new engine blocks desperately needed, the engineering team rushed out to the foundry to hand-rub sand into high-stress areas so more cast iron would integrate into the material. Days before race day, the new engine blocks were finished, but the improved 426 Hemis still needed to be assembled. Hours before the race, the new engines left Highland Park, Michigan. Much to the relief of all involved, the engines were installed just in time, and Chrysler's teams amazingly took first, second, and third place, with Richard Petty finishing first. Richard's Plymouth Belvedere with the 426 Hemi became known as "the elephant" because of its weight, and this engine would play a pivotal role in launching Richard into racing fame. He would go on to win a stunning two hundred races in his career, including seven Daytona 500s, and be crowned with his awesome nickname, "The King." Let's just say . . . engines matter.[2]

Yet, the engine that matters most in any man's life is the one that determines not his speed but his direction. That engine is the heart. Proverbs says, "Everything you do flows from it."[3] In other words, without your heart, you go nowhere and do nothing. Robert Saucy says it well: "The propensities of the new heart are the most powerful force in the believer's life."[4] These words point to an incredibly important truth: you have been made new from the inside out, and your new heart has powerhouse capability and capacity. This truth is most profoundly felt in the heart's ability to receive God and respond to God's leading. And its newness is further expressed by new strength, new prowess, new desires, and new life. The question is, What are you going to do with it?

Your Unfair Advantage

All of this talk about the new heart is built on the assumption that you have made the decision to follow Jesus. If you have, congratulations are in order—your heart is no longer desperately wicked above all things (which is obviously a very good thing). You are not the same person you used to be. Jesus hit the eject button on the culture of hell that had overrun your inner life. He transformed your heart into a sacred space that the Holy Spirit actually wants to inhabit. That might not mean much to you now, but by the end of this chapter, it will.

Whether you are completely conscious of what has shifted inside of you or not, the fact is, you are not the same person you once were. The core of who you are has been made new, and you now have what you need to live the lionhearted life God created you for. This is not something to simply acknowledge with a yawn and move on from. It's like He dropped the first ever 426 Hemi inside of you to power you toward divine design and destiny. You could and should think about it this way: God has literally given you an unfair advantage. Fair is getting what you deserve. Grace is getting what you don't deserve. When God made you new on the inside, He gave you what you didn't have any rightful claim to and something most of humanity doesn't have. The apostle Paul said it this way: "by grace you have been saved."[5] What happened to you didn't happen because of you. You didn't check the right boxes. You didn't qualify for some special upgrade. You didn't make it happen.

The majority of people are living with hearts that are dead and deformed by sin. They are living with hearts that are still desperately wicked. They may not realize it, but they cannot walk with God, know God, continuously experience His presence and power, or live out His plan for their lives until they get the new heart that you have. Listen, God doesn't save you and transform you just to get you ready for heaven—He saves you and transforms you to empower you for a way of life that would be impossible otherwise. He has enabled you to live out the version of manhood men were intended to live out before Satan, sin, and death disastrously interfered. This means that the version of "masculinity" being pushed by culture is a demonic counterfeit. It defaces the way that men were uniquely created to be carriers of the image of God.[6] Whether it is a version that is domineering, overbearing, arrogant, timid, passive, lazy, anti-responsibility, or selfish—all of these are contrary to biblical manhood, but grace has given you an undeserved advantage.

Why the Hell Got Kicked Out of Your Heart

It doesn't take a rocket scientist to understand that evicting darkness, death, and the demonic from your core is a good thing. But this is just the beginning of what God desires to do in your life. The endgame of Jesus's life, death, and resurrection wasn't just to get you out of the negative. The goal wasn't just to get you back to zero. He wasn't just getting rid of your sin, He was completely rewiring from the inside out how life can work for you. God was giving you the power to accelerate into His plan and purpose for your life in ways that weren't even possible prior to receiving your new heart. The problem is that too many men never tap into the full potential of what God has done in them.

Now, we are about to tell you something that we hope doesn't cause any of you to abandon ship on this book or lose faith in us. Though the opening of this chapter may have fooled you, neither of us is a car guy. Not even a little bit. We have friends who are. We admire their mechanical acumen, but we, sadly, don't possess their automotive prowess. We don't even change our own oil. Our car-loving friends can't help talking about the capabilities of whatever they are driving, working on, or dreaming about. In fact, one of our friends has been building one vehicle for almost a decade! Neither of us has seen the beast he is building in person, but any time we hang together we get all of the updates. Because that's how car guys are. They are literal evangelists for the gospel of horsepower. They can tell you details about the engines under their hoods that you wouldn't think were even possible to know or that you would want to know. They are constantly tweaking and tuning and upgrading, and when they figure out a way to go faster, they cannot wait to demonstrate their car's newfound capacity.

Not too long ago, we showed up at a restaurant with our wives to meet two other couples for dinner, and the car they arrived in had just been named the fastest car *MotorTrend* had ever tested in its 0–60 mph ranking. As we headed toward our table, one of the guys said, "Do you want to go for a ride right now?" And just like that, we abandoned our wives. Who needs food when you can have speed? For these guys, when the car is "scary fast," they have only just begun.

Your new heart has capacity you have never even dreamed of. It can help you go places in life and in your walk with God and experience His power in ways that you haven't begun to imagine, but fully utilizing this engine at the center of your life doesn't happen by accident. In fact, if you are not aware of the power of the heart you now possess, you are destined to continue to live life based on the capabilities of the vastly inferior heart you used to have.[7] Many Christian men shrink back from the lionhearted existence that God has hardwired them for because they are misinformed or uninformed about the engine that they have been equipped with.

Driving Like a Grandma

What do we mean when we say they are misinformed? Someone at some point on their journey has led them down the wrong path in their thinking about the core of who they are. They were taught things about themselves that are simply not true.

How do you know if you are misinformed? The major way that misguided thinking manifests itself is when men view their hearts as saved but not really new. In other words, they identify as a follower of Jesus but live absent of the power that Jesus has given them because they still see their inner life as fatally flawed and desperately wicked even though that is no longer true. They still see the words of Jeremiah 17:9, "The human heart is the most deceitful of all things, and desperately wicked" (NLT), as an accurate picture of who they are, even as a follower of Jesus. That's a big problem.

If that is your view of yourself, then you will subconsciously excuse yourself from holiness by pointing to your desperately wicked heart. You will operate out of the assumption that you can't walk in the power, authority, or victory that the Bible makes clear is part of the Christian life. In other words, because you are misinformed you will opt out of what Jesus died and rose to make possible in you and through you, and you will unknowingly opt in to a version of masculinity that delights the devil. You have to decide to stop looking at yourself and living like nothing really happened at the core of who you are when God saved you! You have to stop thinking like the old you is still you. This is critical because if you lose sight of the new heart God has given you, it can lead to hopelessness and depression. You might think, "I don't know if God can change me," or "I will always be this way." These untrue thoughts and beliefs about the transforming work God has done in your heart are like weights that will slow you down and keep you from being able to change.

This misinformed or uninformed self-perception perpetuates an anemic version of manhood. If you don't fully grasp what God has done inside of you when He gave you the heart transplant that we talked about in chapter 3, then you will be like Grandma driving 20 miles per hour down the highway behind the wheel of a Lamborghini. Not only is that sad, it's also dangerous. We are not calling you a grandma, but it could be that you are living your life like that by not accessing the potential of your new heart. When you misunderstand what you have, then you don't operate in the power God has given you. You feel stuck or, at the very least, slow. The truth is, with a new heart, you CAN change. You can be kind to your wife. You can be patient with your kids. You can get out of the pit of sexual sin. You can change the way you talk. You can forgive that person who hurt you. You can live like a lion. Knowing what God gave you in the new heart He placed inside of you is essential to experiencing everything else He wants to do in your life. Yes, your heart used to be the worst part of you, the epicenter of your brokenness, but the new heart you were given is now the best part of who you are if you choose to maximize it as the new engine God gave you.

The Heart: Command Central

Our world is clueless about the heart. The word is thrown around so much that most people, even most Christians, have no idea what "the heart" (biblically defined) actually is. People usually talk about it in a vague metaphorical sense but with little or no concrete understanding. They operate off a fuzzy assumption that it must have something to do with a person's emotions. Yet, Dane Ortlund is right on target in saying, "When the Bible speaks of the heart, whether Old Testament or New, it is not speaking of our emotional life only but of the central animating center of all we do. It is what gets us out of bed in the morning and what we daydream about as we drift off to sleep. It is our motivation headquarters. The heart, in biblical terms, is not part of who we are but the center of who we are."[8] When you survey Scriptures that speak to what makes a person, the picture of what the heart is and does becomes clear and concrete. But we don't just want you to take our word for it, so we are going to dive a bit deeper (but we promise not to hold you under too long).

What the Heart Is

Hebrew is the original language of the Old Testament, and the Hebrew word for heart (*leb* or *lebab*) shows up in the Bible 858 times. The Old Testament scholar Hans Walter Wolff writes that "the most important word in the vocabulary of Old Testament anthropology is generally translated heart."[9] Or you could state it a bit more bluntly, like the theologian Robert Saucy puts it: "the word heart is the most significant term for understanding the person."[10] Biblically, you can't know who you are without understanding your heart. Now, you may be tempted to say, "Well, that's the Old Testament. The people of that time had a more antiquated view of the world." Not so fast. The same God inspired the entire Bible, so the same level of truthfulness permeates the book from cover to cover. And the New Testament talks about the heart proportionally as often as the Old Testament.[11] Bottom line: the Bible has a lot to say about the heart because it touches every area of your life.

We need to clear up some muddiness here. Words like *heart*, *soul*, and *spirit* are used in casual conversation like we are all talking about the same thing, but if you ask a few follow-up questions, it becomes clear that pretty much nobody knows what they are talking about. So, what does the Bible say about what makes a man? To answer this question, we once again need to go back to the beginning.

In Genesis 2, we get the essential ingredients that make a human being: "Then the LORD God formed the man from the dust of the ground. He breathed the breath of life into the man's nostrils, and the man became a living person [literally translated 'soul']."[12] At your most basic, you are the union of dust and the breath of God. Every person who has ever lived is a combination of their physical body and their immaterial spirit, the total package being a living soul.[13] The word *soul* signifies the whole person. You are not a body with a soul. The soul is not what you have. *It is who you are!* Think of it this way: There's the material part of you, made up of bones, muscles, nerves, organs, cells, and so on—the part you were taking care of when you went to the gym this morning (or not) and when you decided to forgo fast food for lunch yesterday. Then there's the spirit part of you that no microscope can see or examine but is just as real. Together they are the soul, the whole you, with the heart at the center. So, when God saves your soul, He is saving your body and your spirit. He saves the whole person.

The Bible says that if you die before Jesus returns, your spirit goes to be with God, but when Christ comes back, your body will be raised from the dead because that is an essential part of who you are (1 Cor. 15:52; 2 Cor. 5:8). So, when you are at a funeral and someone points to the lifeless body in the casket and says that's not Uncle Bob (or whoever), they may be trying to offer comfort, but what they are saying isn't actually true. The fact is, that body in that casket is Uncle Bob. It's as much Uncle Bob as his spirit that has gone to be with Jesus. It's just not *all* of Uncle Bob. Until Jesus comes back, he (Bob) will be an incomplete person. Because, like any other person who has ever lived, he is the combination of body and spirit as a living soul with his heart at the center of who he is.

Some people will say God only cares about the immaterial part of you. In both Hinduism and Buddhism, the body only serves as temporary, disposable housing for the soul. Others will argue that all that matters is the physical. Secular culture is obsessed with the body. Christianity inextricably links these two as essential to what it means to be human with the heart functioning as command central of the whole person.

What the Heart Does

There is a place we all must venture to at some point that demands bravery, fortitude, and determination. It's not a pilgrimage for the timid or the easily flustered. It will test almost every part of you that can be tested. You will leave physically, mentally, and emotionally depleted, but when your quest is complete, you will have the satisfaction that you survived. What is this hallowed quest? Your trip to the DMV.

Now, we want to be clear, the problem with the Department of Motor Vehicles is not the people. If you work at the DMV, we salute you for your courage. The problem is the process. You enter and take a number. The somber atmosphere is filled with an air of stress mixed with boredom. You sit waiting for your number to be called, 99.9 percent sure that when your number is finally called, you will be told you are missing something. What is this mysterious "something"? That's impossible to say. All you are sure of is that it will be something the DMV doesn't have but that is absolutely essential to the task you are trying to complete. What you really needed was a piece of paper that you can only get from an office at the county courthouse that is conveniently open 1:15–1:45 p.m. on the second Tuesday of every other month. Does this sound familiar? What should take five minutes turns into hours because everything isn't in one place.

That's not the heart. Everything is in one place—your thoughts, beliefs, memories, loves, hates, choices, desires, and dreams are interconnected and come out of your heart. This truth surfaced at the start of our journey, but it bears repeating.

The Heart Is for Understanding

You think from the heart. Listen to this sad assessment Moses made of the people of Israel: "the LORD has not given you a heart to understand or eyes to see or ears to hear."[14] Just like the eyes are for seeing and the ears are for hearing, the heart is for understanding. Proverbs 15:14 says, "The discerning heart seeks knowledge, but the mouth of a fool feeds on folly." The healthy heart is knowledge-hungry. It thrives on processing helpful information. And Scripture doesn't just say God's Word judges our hearts, it judges "thoughts and attitudes of the heart."[15] So, when Death Cab for Cutie opines,

> I'm in a war of head versus heart
> And it's always this way
> My head is weak, my heart always speaks
> Before I know what it will say[16]

we have to say, "Not so fast," because you don't have a smart head and a stupid heart. Your head and your heart are inextricably connected.

The Heart Controls Emotions

But one of you is saying, "Wait a minute! Aren't we supposed to love God with all our heart?" Whoever said that gets a gold star! The Bible says that not only does the heart think, but it is also the internal address of your emotions. Joy and sadness, love and hate, tenacity and fear, and any other emotion you want to name can be found in your heart. Jesus said to the disciples, "Do not let your hearts be troubled."[17] In Psalm 22:14, David wrote that his heart "has turned to wax; it has melted within me." Isaiah talked about a glad heart.[18] The Bible is full of references to the heart's emotional capacity. But perhaps what is most important for you to realize is that the heart is the place of decision.

The Heart Is the Place of Decision

King David said that God gave him "his heart's desire."[19] In the New Testament, the apostle Paul talked about his "heart's desire" in Romans 10:1. But the heart is not just the place of desire, it's also the headquarters of decision-making. A guy named Barnabas, a close companion of the apostle Paul, encouraged some of the first Christians to follow God with "resolute heart."[20] Resolute—this means the heart is where you resolve to not back down. It's also the place where your drive and motivation come from. In fact, God says he will reveal the "motives of men's hearts."[21]

Maybe right about now you're thinking, "Great, now I know what my heart is and does. What do I do with that?" The reason for this brief biblical survey of what the heart does is so that you know just how powerful the engine God has given you is. It controls your smallest desires and your biggest dreams. It informs your self-perceptions and the way you perceive everything else around you. It drives your decisions and therefore your destiny. As Dane Ortlund writes, "Our heart is what defines and directs us."[22] Nothing matters more than your heart, because your life, your plans, your hopes, your habits, and your future will all ultimately only be as good as your heart. This is why God's gift of a new heart that the Spirit of God lives in is such a big deal—your life gets a divinely engineered core, and the Holy Spirit is the fuel that enables that new engine to perform at its highest level. When the heart gets right, everything else is freed up to line up with God's plan and purpose for your life. Living life at the speed of your divinely determined potential only happens when your inner life is functioning at optimal capacity. Yet, as astounding as this may sound, the combination of a new heart and the presence of the Holy Spirit is just the *baseline* for going where God wants to take you. Because this engine doesn't just have all of the capabilities we have already discussed, it also has the capacity to grow.

Heart Work Is Hard Work

If the image that just popped into your head is of the Grinch's heart growing three sizes, you are not alone. It's too iconic to be avoided. And don't get us wrong, every Christmas we celebrate the Grinch's sudden transformation. The sad part about that picture is that it is very much in keeping with our culture's narrative about the heart—it's cartoonish, sappy, and childish. The reason this visual is problematic for every man reading this book is that it causes you to dismiss the importance, power, and potential of the real-life acceleration of what God wants to do on the inside of you. Here's the other reality that is in play as we talk about the growth of your heart: we all know deep down that "heart work is indeed hard work."[23] But the growth on the other side of that work is worth it. Not easy, but worth it.

As we have looked at the expansive capacity of the heart that Scripture highlights, maybe this thought has crossed your mind: "I'm a Christian, but what you are describing doesn't match how I feel about what's happening on the inside." Exactly. That shouldn't surprise any of us. The new heart has enormous capacity and potential, but it is also very much like the tiny seed of a giant sequoia. Even the General Sherman tree, whose height is only thirteen feet shorter than the US Capitol Building, started as a seed the size of a pinhead. And yet, here's the even more startling reality: sequoia seeds stay in their pine cones for nearly twenty years before seeing the light of day, and it's the heat from natural forest fires that helps release the seed to begin growing. God has planted a sequoia in your soul, but that sequoia only begins to grow when you respond to the Holy Spirit lighting a fire in your soul to start cultivating the seed. The heart needs to mature. When you start following Jesus, the Bible compares you to a newborn baby (probably not the way you prefer to think of yourself), but that also explains why your heart may not seem like it's living up to its potential.[24] All of that begins to change as the fire of the Holy Spirit moves you to start intentionally doing the work that leads to growth. So, where does that work begin?

Staying in Tune

One of the least sexy but absolutely necessary parts of being a musician is constantly tuning and retuning your instrument. We both took guitar lessons for years, and one of the first things we learned to do was tune our instruments. As aspiring rock stars (sadly, our budding musical careers never really took off), we quickly learned that guitars don't stay in tune. There are many reasons that guitars go out of tune—something as mundane as the weather, a lack of use, or that it got bumped. But the fact is no matter how cool you think you are (we thought we were so cool), until you learn to keep your guitar in tune, you are going to sound terrible, and your playing is going to be painful to the people around you. The same is true with your heart. You have to learn to tune your heart because your heart can go out of tune and, if left unchecked, it can cause all kinds of pain for you and those around you. The good news for young guitarists is that all you have to do is go down to your local Guitar Center and pick up a tuner to begin fixing the problem.

Keeping your heart in tune is not so easy. First, it can be hard to tell that it is out of tune. Second, we mask our sad-sounding internal instrument by at least looking the part. Third, we are surrounded by influences that give false information about how in tune our hearts actually are. The only way to know the state of your heart is to constantly let God tune and retune your heart. It's consistent exposure to God's Word, God's presence, and God's people that lets you know what's actually happening on the inside. Heart work is hard work because it's never done and it's always going to take humility to do it. You will never be able to set it and forget it. You will never reach the point of always and forever being in tune. You will never be able to switch to autopilot. You will always need the Bible to light up the dark corners of your heart. You will always need time with God, in both daily private prayer and weekly gatherings with other Jesus followers. You will always need men in your life who can call you out, who can tell you that something is off. And it will always take humility to listen, but as you lean into the tuning and retuning process, your heart will grow, and you will progressively unlock the potential that it possesses.

Listening is the key. This is why one of the wisest men who ever lived (he literally wrote the book on wisdom), King Solomon, made this his number one prayer: "Here's what I want: Give me a God-listening heart."[25] This is our most consistent prayer, and you should make it yours. Because there is no lionhearted living without listening. It's the moment-by-moment desire to hear God speak that will ultimately determine your ability to walk in His best for your life. If you have never prayed the prayer that King Solomon prayed, now would be a good time to start. It's a request. All you have to say is what he said: "Here's what I want: Give me a God-listening heart. Amen."

Now that you understand the power of your new heart and you have positioned yourself to stay in tune with God, you could think that it's all going to be smooth sailing. Wouldn't that be nice! We would love to tell you that all of your battles are in the rearview mirror, but the truth is that there is still combat on the horizon. Your new heart is not immune to the assault of Satan or sin, but it is fit for the fight. You have been transformed and empowered by the Holy Spirit to withstand the onslaughts that will undoubtedly be part of the days ahead. Now it's time to to know how you will be attacked so that you can win the battles that every lionhearted man will face.

05

The He(ART) of Self-Deception

If we do not know our hearts, it will
be as if we knew nothing at all.

Charles Bridges

Search me, O God, and know my heart!
Try me and know my thoughts!

Psalm 139:23 ESV

Why would the Federal Bureau of Investigation pay a con
man $150,000, plus bonuses? Because Mel was just that
good. He had already successfully conned people out of
millions.

Mel Weinberg's con was simple. He promised people
who couldn't get traditional loans that for a nonrefundable

$1,000 deposit he could secure a loan for them from investors. The catch was the investors didn't exist, and his real plan was to pocket the money and ghost his clients. He did this again and again. Trading on people's hopes was incredibly lucrative. At its height, his scheme was making $1 million a year. His scam worked because he understood human nature. He liked to say, "Everybody has to have hope. That's why most people don't turn us in to the cops. They keep hopin' we're for real."[1]

In 1977, his con game caught up to him. He was indicted for fraud and was headed to prison when the FBI had an idea. Instead of putting him behind bars, why not put him to work? Weinberg agreed to go undercover, and a new con began. The FBI paired him up with agents posing as the representatives of a fabulously wealthy Arab sheikh and started offering bribes to unsuspecting elected officials. These lawmakers said they could get the sheikhs residency in the United States for the right price.[2] Over the course of a few years, the partnership between a con artist and the FBI led to the arrest of one senator, six congressmen, and more than a dozen corrupt officials. Mel had mastered taking advantage of the nearly universal human tendency to be self-deceived.

For all those who think they are not self-deceived and are contemplating skipping this chapter to "leave it to those poor souls who actually need it," you are probably the most likely candidate to be *in* a place of self-deception and therefore a place of self-sabotage. A person who is not currently living under self-deception has been there at some point and by God's grace has gotten out. However, he is under no illusion that he could not fall into the same trap again. He knows everyone at one time or another falls prey to lies he sells to himself, and knowing how easily it can happen, he keeps his guard up and his senses strong.

He also knows self-deception is deadly; if he is not vigilant, it will derail and destroy who he wants to become and who God created him to be. And the scariest part is, he won't even see it coming.

Detached from Reality

One of the best things about being a dad is that your kids force you back into the realm of imagination. As adults, we seem to slowly lose our ability and desire to make believe. We let Hollywood do the heavy lifting for us, so that we can sink into the sofa with sugar and salt coursing through our bodies. That's as close as most men get to imagining. For our kids, watching is okay but the real joy is found in entering another world populated by their imaginations with invading armies, ten-story castles, supersonic airplanes, and whatever else their minds can dream up. Our kids have recently discovered Zorro, and we're not talking late '90s Antonio Banderas Zorro. We are talking about the adventures of Diego de la Vega from the 1950s in all their black-and-white glory. True, the storytelling is formulaic, but our kids are mesmerized by Zorro's unending ability to get the jump on the unwitting villains. Yet they can only watch the sword fights for so long before they are compelled to pick up their own toy swords or sticks and battle against one another. Not only do they want to duel one another but they desperately want Dad to join the fight. And so we happily enter the world of fantasy, unrestrained by the confines of reality.

That periodic detachment from the real world is not only fun, it's healthy, especially when you are traversing alternate universes alongside your kids. But as fun as that may be, you can't live there. At some point, the make-believe comes to an end. In fact, it would be a big problem if our kids only lived life as swashbuckling characters in league with an imaginary vigilante. Here's the sad truth: many men willfully choose to view themselves, their motivations, their decisions, and their actions through a lens that is just as detached from reality as our kids inhabiting the world of Zorro. And both the detachment and the deception are constant threats to a lionhearted life, and if we are not vigilant in guarding against them, we will inevitably succumb to them.

Have you ever stopped and asked yourself why one of the prayers that King David, the most famous king in Israel's history, is best known for is about inviting God to search his heart? It goes like this: "Search me, O God, and know my heart; test me and know my anxious thoughts. Point out anything in me that offends you, and lead me along the path of everlasting life."[3] That's a gutsy prayer. Apparently, David had enough self-awareness to know that it is very possible to have things in your heart that you don't even know are there. He is asking God to show him what he can't see, what he hasn't wanted to see, what he has covered up and excused and ignored and tolerated. For the most part, all of us want to believe we are doing the right things for the right reasons—or at least we are trying.

We want to evaluate our lives at the level of our intentions, not our actions. "I am trying to walk in purity and guard my thoughts . . ." but your browsing history, Netflix account, and late-night scrolling on social media tell a different tale. "I am honest . . ." but you know there is a string of half-truths you have let spool out in conversations over the last week to bolster your image. "I am a person of integrity . . ." but the privacy screen on your phone isn't just for hiding memos attached to emails from the office. "I am wholeheartedly committed to following Jesus and making Him the center of my life . . ." but your time in God's house and in God's Word are inconsistent at best. Your self-assessment is detached from reality. We would prefer to believe that our intentions are what's most important. We live from a mantra that it's what we *meant* to do that actually matters. All of this speaks to our preference for nonreality. That's why David's prayer is incredibly gutsy—because he is asking God to undo any illusions that he has fostered in his own heart and mind that have allowed him to feel good about the status quo.

Now, we realize that it could seem we have turned on the condemnation full blast, that we want you to feel bad about yourself. Our point is quite the opposite. We don't want you to feel good when things aren't good. The goal is not to condemn but to disrupt destructive comfort. We want to shake you out of any lethargy in areas where you have been lulled into complacency, robbing you of the best that God wants and has for you. Only you know if that's something you really want. There are plenty of men who prefer la-la land, but you should know that the Bible has a name for that kind of man. They are fools. Proverbs 14:8 says, "The prudent understand where they are going, but fools deceive themselves" (NLT). Notice that in this verse Solomon says that fools not only con themselves but they lose in the deal. They swindle themselves out of any aware-ness of where they are going. Maybe you know some-one like this. Though they have done little actual work or haven't made the sacrifices necessary for success, they are absolutely convinced things are going great. Their idea is about to take off. Their big breakthrough is just around the corner. The world is their oyster. And yet, everyone around them is painfully aware of what they can't seem to see. This is why reality-detached living is so detrimen-tal to the desire for a lionhearted life. It is essential that you understand where your desires, motivations, patterns, relationships, and actions are actually taking you.

Deconstructing Your Self-Deception

The physicist Richard Feynman famously said, "The first principle is that you must not fool yourself, and you are the easiest person to fool."[4] Self-deception may be the most difficult kind of lie for a man to unravel because we have often linked the lie to other beliefs that fortify our broken perspective, beliefs we would rather not jettison. For instance, you have blissfully believed that your wan-dering eyes and lustful thoughts are simply part of life, and you shrug these tendencies off as something every guy deals with and nobody ever really breaks free from. Then often what accompanies those thoughts—excuses—is the notion that you don't need to strive for purity because that pursuit is a lost cause. And since every dude is in the same boat, there is really no reason to tell anyone about the images and fantasies that populate your mind. What good would that do, anyway? Why fight the way you are hardwired? The problem with allowing your heart to be a haven for this kind of deception is that it destroys so much of what God desires to do in you, through you, and for you. That's why, with gut-level passion, the long-dead pastor and theologian John Owen reaches a fever-pitch in his warning about this way of thinking:

> The world is at this day full of poor withering [Christians].
> How few are there that walk in any beauty or glory! How
> barren, how useless are they, for the most part! Amongst
> the many reasons that may be assigned of this sad estate, it
> may justly be feared that this is none of the least effectual—
> many men harbor spirit-devouring lusts in their [hearts],
> that lie as worms at the root of their obedience, and cor-
> rode and weaken it day by day. All graces, all the ways and
> means whereby any graces may be exercised and improved,
> are prejudiced by this means; and as to any success, God
> blasts such men's undertakings.[5]

Don't let his cumbersome phrasing keep this quote from sinking in. Owen doesn't mince words. Though his target is lust, you could just as easily apply this warning to any other hellish con that could infiltrate your heart. When was the last time you were told that as a Christian you could be "useless" or that God would "blast" what you are trying to do? Owen is getting in your face. He under-stands just how deadly deception can be, which is why it has to be dealt with.

The good news is when you choose to confront the nucleus of your self-deception in one area of your life, all the other dominos begin to fall. The house of cards you created to make yourself feel good about living a sub-lionhearted existence comes crashing down. As a character in George Saunders's book *Liberation Day* muses, "Sometimes in life the foundation upon which one stands will give a tilt, and everything one has previously believed and held dear will begin sliding about, and suddenly all things will seem strange and new."[6] That may sound like an overstatement, but we would contend that the choice to challenge the false narrative you have made space for in your heart will touch every part of your life. Dare we say this chapter could be so transformative that everything will seem strange and new in a lionhearted sort of way? So, where to begin?

It starts with knowing you can be deceived. Go back to what King David prayed. His cry to God is "Search me!" The implication of this prayer is that there are things below the surface of his life that even he cannot see, but God can. He also understands how important it is to get God's perspective on what is happening at the core of who he is. This is where freedom from self-deception starts for every one of us. As Robert Saucy writes, "The truth is that other thoughts and attitudes deep in our hearts—of which we are not fully conscious—are actually driving our life."[7] You will never live a lionhearted life without a fierce commitment to knowing what is driving your desires and decisions, and consequently your direction, because if you don't know, then you are probably being driven by the wrong things. King David was a guy who killed bears and lions and, most famously, a giant, but it took even more bravery for him to acknowledge before God that he might have things inside of him that shouldn't be there, that he couldn't even see. Here's a question for you: What kinds of things do you think might be deep down in your heart that God needs to be invited to search out? (Spoiler alert: If your answers come easily, they are most likely wrong.)

Recently we read about a Ukrainian sniper who claimed that he had set a record for the longest kill shot fired in action. He said that his bullet had traveled 2.36 miles. The sniper had hidden, waited, and fired without even the slightest awareness on his target's part that ammunition had left the barrel of his rifle.[8] Self-deception works that way. Often you don't know it's there until it's too late. It comes disguised. It lurks in overconfidence, insecurity, and other forms of pride. Here are just a few of the ways it manifests itself in our lives.

Victim Mentality

Self-deception is present when you can only see yourself as a victim: a victim because of your family, your marriage, your economic situation, your relationship with your boss. You name it, and self-deception will easily conjure up a victim label if you want one. This is not to say that people are not legitimately victimized by others. That's not what we are talking about here. We are dealing with a mentality that you have allowed to frame your existence. In a marriage, this happens when you start overemphasizing your needs and underemphasizing your wife's. It's the internal soundtrack that goes something like this: "I am the one who carries all the pressure around here. Why am I always the one who has to do everything? All she does is complain and nitpick." Victimhood in marriage is like cuffing a ball and chain to your ankle and jumping into an ocean of misery. It's catastrophic.

And it usually starts with a lot of self-talk about fairness. You feel you deserve better. You should get more of the credit. You wish people (namely, your spouse) would stop expecting so much. And all that self-talk in turn leads to a string of self-justifications. You feel justified in looking at porn, masturbating, having a drink to take the edge off, or engaging in long conversations with the new girl at the office. You constantly think about how you are being treated, how you are not heard or cared for. You are a victim, and therefore your lack of lionheartedness is justifiable. How could you be lionhearted, with everyone picking at you constantly? But the problem is, if you are a victim in your marriage, you are driving your wife and your family nowhere but around a miserable cul-de-sac of your personal woes. This can only go on for so long, until your marriage runs out of gas, or your wife runs for the hills. People will talk about the missing spark that once characterized their relationship, and often what put the fire out can be traced back to a victim mentality. It's a bad deal.

Marriage isn't the only place this shows up. Victimhood is a badge that men can subconsciously wear in other areas. If you have a victim mindset financially, you will blame and embitter yourself toward those who have what you don't. If you are a victim at work, you will do less than you are capable of, indirectly or directly talk disparagingly about your boss, and feel wronged by a laundry list of slights related to your pay, your hours, the advancement of others, and more.

Once again, there are people who are victims in the world, and you may be one of them. Maybe your wife or boss has wronged you. That's tragic, but the answer is not to play the victim but to lean into the power and potential of the new heart that God has given you, to live the lionhearted existence you were meant and made for. This is not so you can attack people who hurt you like a wild lion would. You are lionhearted so you can kill that poisonous root of bitterness in your soul that the enemy wants you to water and feed until it covers every part of your life like kudzu vines. Don't do it. You are not a victim; you are a conqueror. You may not feel like it, but you were created to live above the pettiness that defines the world of a victim. Remember, a victim always justifies tearing down, but a lionhearted person builds up. Maybe you need God to search your heart and help you remove the venom of victimhood from your heart.

Self-Righteousness

Self-deception also shows up as camouflaged self-righteousness. If lionheartedness had one polar opposite, it might just be self-righteousness. Self-righteousness is a plague as old as the first brothers on Planet Earth, Cain and Abel, who made up the first sibling rivalry, which ended in a murder because of—you guessed it—self-righteousness. And just like Cain killed Abel because Abel was actually righteous, self-righteousness beckons you to undermine, malign, and mistreat any person in your life who actually has a real and vibrant walk with God. You will also (as much as possible) crush any desire for God in those around you. Why? Because you are spiritually insecure. How are you self-righteous? You are "spiritual," but primarily in relationship to yourself, not your relationship with God. You engage in lots of self-sacrifice without real obedience, because obedience starts with humility, and the "self" part of self-righteousness will have none of that. The real deception is that this faux righteousness has the look and feel of spiritual leadership. It can even produce a cheap imitation of lionheartedness because of its piety and sacrifice, but it's based on a lie. It's got a rotten core. It's garbage. Self-righteousness is really about image control and people control. It holds people—including us—to unattainable standards without compassion or any concern for actual spiritual life, while never feeling any need to personally repent. As Leonard Ravenhill says, "The self-righteous never apologize."[9] The prophet Obadiah puts it this way: "The pride of your heart has deceived you."[10]

The self-righteous brand of self-deception puts its own effort above all else. It comes from a deep insecurity inside a soul that is hollow. Note: If this is you, you might be reading this right now and thinking it applies to someone else. Step back and, with humility, begin again. You might be self-deceived. Perhaps you force spirituality, manufacturing it instead of modeling a passionate pursuit of deeper communion with God and asking God to produce that passion in you where you don't see it. You talk about all the bad people in the world, using words like *idiots* and *morons* to describe them. You struggle to have peace in your relationships with the people around you because you don't have peace on the inside, and it nags at you. You feel like you are supposed to have it all together (and might even be junior varsity at convincing people that you do), but you know you don't.

The first king of Israel, Saul, suffered from this self-deception throughout his reign. He would do things that were seemingly spiritual, but he didn't have a walk with God. At one point he was about to lead his men into a battle against his archnemesis, the Philistines, and he knew he needed God's help but he didn't want to do things God's way. Instead of waiting for the prophet Samuel to seek God on his behalf, he did his own thing. His actions had the trappings of spirituality, but he had little regard for seeking God on the basis of his relationship with Him.[11]

This gave his life and spirituality a hollow ring that left him frustrated and the people around him perplexed. At one point in the middle of a military campaign, Saul decided to call his soldiers to fast. The problem was that he said nothing about prayer. So now his soldiers were just hungry. Because of Saul's actions, Scripture says his people were "in distress." Even Saul's own son knew his dad's directive didn't make any sense.[12] This is a picture of the way spiritual activity detached from spiritual substance simply confuses and demoralizes the people around you. If you have read about Saul's life and legacy, you have likely noticed that he was just off. This type of self-deception is not only found in conservative Christian circles, it's alive and well everywhere—and it kills.

Unfortunately, this is one of the hardest self-deceptions to overcome because it also breeds a hard heart. Therefore, if you think even for a second that this could be you, stop and ask God to reveal your lack of relationship with Him. But get ready. Often, He will use someone in your life who is *way* less disciplined and less "spiritual" to show your actual spiritual poverty. Humble yourself and repent. Stop telling everyone else how things should be done and instead pray for them to love Jesus, experience His grace and presence, and have His peace. Finally, when Jesus asks you to do something, then *do* it! Don't tell other people to do it. You do it, even if it's embarrassing. God opposes the proud but gives grace to the humble. If you want to be lionhearted, you can't live in the self-deception of self-righteousness.

Spiritual Lethargy

If this is you, you probably know you are spiritually lethargic. You might be thinking, "If I know then I am technically not self-deceived." Ah, but the deception comes in when you say, "I might be spiritually lethargic, but I am going to step it up one day." The glorious "one day." Some magical day in the future. The day when the baby starts sleeping through the night. The day when the pace at work finally becomes manageable. The day when you finish your degree. The day when you add a few more employees. The day when you just aren't so dang tired.

Stop. That magical day is a myth. The "one day" you have set as a hypothetical target for the acceleration of your spiritual walk is like a dream that you can never catch. It's not a real day. Oh, it seems real. That is, it seems real if you are living in self-deception. Honestly, this might sound offensive for two guys you don't know to tell you that you are making excuses. But you need to hear it from somebody: Your reasoning is built on the false premise that one day it will get easier to do what you know you should be doing today. We're sorry to destroy your fantasy. The fact is lionhearted men don't live in the "one day" world. They know "one day" never comes. And so they stop making excuses and start going after God now. They do what matters now. They start passionately pursuing God now.

Spiritual lethargy is so damaging because you know exactly what you need to do. You just don't do it. So, in moments where you realize how you are really doing, there is a lot of shame and guilt. But here's the problem: shame and guilt will get you nowhere. Shame and guilt move you farther from being a lionhearted man. What you need is humility, repentance (i.e., change), and responsibility. It's that last one that's really the difference maker: taking responsibility is the key to moving out of spiritual lethargy. This is why it is so hard. Many people equate shame with responsibility, and therefore reject it altogether. Think about the guy who knows he needs to lose weight, but every time he thinks about it, a narrative of self-loathing kicks into high gear in his head and submarines any positive movement toward change. Responsibility is not beating yourself up—that's shame. Shame puts your shortcomings on repeat with the volume turned up until your ears bleed.

Taking responsibility for your pursuit of Christ has the opposite effect. Shame will have you treating your relationship with God like a DIY project that you have no hope of ever getting done. Responsibility is what the apostle Paul is talking about when he says, "Continue to work out your salvation with fear and trembling, for it is God who works in you to will and to act in order to fulfill his good purpose."[13] You actually disarm the shame of spiritual lethargy by taking responsibility, no longer making it all about you, and instead making it about cooperating with what God is doing in your life.

These are just a few of the most prominent ways we construct narratives to deceive ourselves. Yet, the truth is you could easily create an encyclopedia to catalog the lies that people allow themselves to believe. Every lie leads the men who buy into it farther from living lionhearted. All of us are going somewhere, but going somewhere good and becoming the lionhearted man God destined you to be doesn't happen by accident. As we once heard John Maxwell say, "No one ever drifts to a desired destination. You drift until you wake up and say 'oh, crap.'"[14] Going somewhere good requires the intentional undoing of deception.

Undoing Deception

As we have already pointed out, King David provides a road map for dealing with deception that can infiltrate our hearts, and when it comes to undoing deception, he tells us exactly where to start. Go to God. This sounds too simple but, like so many foundational truths of the Christian life, it *is* simple. Since life began on Planet Earth, men have avoided taking this very step. Adam, our greatest grandpa, was the first man to ever walk with God, and he was the first man to ever have to deal with deception. Satan worked him over, and Adam took the bait. Then God came looking for him. Do you want to take a wild guess at what he did? It doesn't take a Bible scholar to figure this one out.

He hid. Genesis 3:8 says, "The man and his wife heard the LORD God walking about in the garden. So they hid from the LORD God among the trees" (NLT). The visual would be comical if it wasn't so pathetic. Obviously, the trees weren't blocking God's view of Adam and Eve, but we often deal with deception in the same way. We act as if hiding our deceptions from God means He can't see them, which is the same game that Adam was playing and just as sad. The only way to undo deception in your life is by bringing it to God. But even that is a reactive approach to the undoing that needs to happen in your life. Notice that David is going to God and asking that He root out the deceptions that may be actively at work in his heart but that he is oblivious to. The lionhearted life is not hiding until God comes and finds you (and He will)—the lionhearted life is actively asking Him to help you attack any lie that has been allowed to live in your heart undetected.

This proactive posture means you continually invite your Creator to look under the surface of your life. The world is too full of deception for you to naively think that you will be able to navigate life unscathed without giving God full access to search your heart. Yet, it would be a mistake to think that this is something God does absent of your involvement. He wants to include you in the search so that you see what He sees and become better and better at identifying what should have never been granted entry into your heart in the first place. Maybe you have heard people talk about being sensitive to the Holy Spirit and wondered how that happens. Asking God to search your heart is a key component to cultivating that sensitivity in your life. As you regularly invite God to uncover things you have allowed in that displease Him and to root them out, you will find that you more readily hear the Holy Spirit firing warning shots over potential deceptions, alerting you to danger before it ever gains entry to your heart.

Listen to the plea of John Flavel: "Study your hearts, watch your hearts, keep your hearts! . . . All that I beg for is this, that you would step aside oftener to talk with God and your own heart."[15] What is happening on the inside of you has to be an ongoing conversation with your Creator because if it's not a dialogue, you will view God as being out to get you. Your "Search me, O God" prayer will be hesitant, half-hearted, and begrudging. You will pray it out of religious obligation, if you pray it at all. You will be afraid of what He will find and what He will want to do about what He finds. This perspective causes you to prepare for God's inspections like a prison inmate preparing for a guard to flip his cell—not exactly a process you are excited to participate in. The problem with this viewpoint is that it completely misinterprets the motivation behind God searching your heart. Eugene Petersen's paraphrase of the final line of Psalm 139 is "Guide me on the road to eternal life."[16] The end goal of God going through your interior life with a fine-tooth comb is not to induce a guilt trip but to guide you into His perfect plan for your life. He doesn't search your heart as an enforcer seeking to bend your will into submission to His (although He could certainly do that). He comes to illuminate the darkest corners of your heart to empower you to walk in His purpose.

God is well aware of where He wants to take you and what He wants to do through you. He also knows the damage that hiding anything that has deceived you and displeased Him will do to you. Why else would John Flavel add the line, "All that I beg"? His urgent appeal is that none of us would allow anything to destroy what God desires for our life. This is why you undo self-deception. But you are not the only one who can sabotage your ability to live the lionhearted life. Next chapter we will see what the devil is determined to do to derail where God wants to take you.

06

The Heist from Hell

When someone steals your heart not
even the law can help you.

Matshona Dhliwayo

The careless heart is an easy prey to Satan in
the hover of temptation; his principal batteries
are raised against the heart; if he wins that he
wins all, for it commands the whole man.

John Flavel

You could say that it all started in a blacksmith's shop.
The year is 1618, and a baby is born to a blacksmith and his
wife—a baby who would one day attempt to steal the most
prized possession in all of England. His name is Thomas

Blood, no doubt an apt name for a future thief. You can even tell from his seventeenth-century portrait that this guy is up to no good. To us, the arched eyebrow is a dead giveaway.

Illustration by G. Scott, "Colonel Thomas Blood," 1813.

Though young Thomas came from a "good family" (his grandfather was a member of the British Parliament), he had trouble staying out of trouble. Fast-forward a few decades, and Thomas was living in Holland with a price on his head. Having hatched two failed kidnapping attempts, he now, at the age of fifty-two, decided to set his sights higher. His target was the crown jewels (the drip worn by the newly minted king or queen of England during his or her coronation), which have a present-day value of $57 million and were kept in the Tower of London.

Thomas's plot was simple—to make friends with the Edwards family, who protected the king's very expensive hat (apologies to our British readers for calling the king's crown a hat). The plan worked, and on one visit to the Tower of London, Thomas expressed his desire to "cast his eyes" on the treasure locked inside. Mr. Edwards, who guarded the jewels, agreed to give him a private tour, but when the last door had been unlocked, surprise, surprise, Thomas knocked him out with a mallet and stabbed him (he survived). Then Thomas quickly flattened the crown and stuffed it down his pants. Yes, that really happened.

Thomas ran with his pants crammed full of diamonds, pearls, and gold. Mr. Edwards regained consciousness and started screaming, "Murder! Treason!" The thief tried to shoot a guard but missed and was arrested at the Tower's gate. Thomas Blood had to give back the smashed crown and add another foiled plot to his lackluster criminal résumé.[1]

Apparently, Thomas had not accounted for the other guards on duty that day—one guard is good, but one guard is not sufficient if you are serious about protecting something of value. So, all's well that ends well for the crown jewels. But the outcome is not always as sunny when it comes to our hearts, which is exactly why Proverbs 4:23 is critically important for any person who is serious about the health and strength of their interior life.

> Above all else, guard your heart, for everything you do flows from it.[2]

When you see the phrase "guard your heart" in the middle of Proverbs 4:23, you are encountering a phrase that is deceptively simple. Some scholars have helpfully pointed out that the Hebrew expression here indicates the necessity of setting a "double guard" to protect your heart.[3] In fact, one translation of this verse says, "More than all that you guard, guard."[4]

We guard the things that matter to us. We password-protect our phones, computers, Netflix accounts, TikTok accounts, email accounts, and bank accounts. So. Many. Passwords. We set them and reset them because even though we are prone to forget them, we want to protect what we value. We lock our apartments, our houses, and our cars. We pay monthly for antivirus software, home security systems, and identity theft monitoring. We guard what matters to us, which is precisely why Solomon says that our heart deserves a double guard.

The Heist of the Heart

Erwin Lutzer says it well: "We're in a war. We can't plead pacifism. We can't run from the bullets. We can't hide from the bombs. We can't plead medical deferment. If you have never felt the war within, I can't identify."[5] The heart needs a double guard because it is incredibly vulnerable to attack, and those attacks are usually not so easy to see coming. Fatigue has you run-down and short-circuits your ability to make wise decisions. An unexpected loss blindsides you, and suddenly you find yourself thinking and feeling things you never have before. A relationship sours and the concoction of hurt, pain, and frustration seems like more than you can bear. A dream that you once pursued with passionate optimism appears to be dying with each passing day, and it feels like part of you is dying with it. In any one of these scenarios, your heart can end up unguarded or insufficiently guarded.

It is not just the cataclysmic events of life that threaten the heart—it's petty jealousy, tinges of bitterness, little slights, half-truths, and the ever-present push of demands baked into everyday life that threaten to rob us of peace, contentment, joy, and the heart-health necessary for a holistically healthy life.

If you are going to set a double guard, which is clearly vital in light of the barrage of attacks that the heart can fall prey to, what are the specific predators you should be on the lookout for? What or, maybe more accurately, who will inevitably lay siege to the core of all you are?

The Usual Suspect

You have an enemy. This is not a generic statement about a human relationship that has soured, though most of us will encounter people along the journey who are antagonistic, hostile, and maybe even violently opposed to what we stand for. Those aren't the enemies we should be most concerned about. They may wish the worst for you or even actively work against you, but they will never be as cunning, studied, or strategic as your ultimate enemy. Even the people who are hell-bent on your destruction are never going to be the biggest threat to your heart. The Bible says hell was created for the thief we should be alert to. Peter is quite clear about this when he writes,

> Stay alert! Watch out for your great enemy, the devil. He prowls around like a roaring lion, looking for someone to devour.[6]

The devil or Satan is not just an enemy, he is your *great* enemy. The name "Satan" means "adversary," and the term "devil" means "the accuser, the slanderer." This very clear warning from Peter reminds us that he plays for keeps.[7] The devil's desire for you and every follower of Jesus is bluntly summarized by New Testament scholar Karen Jobes: "The goal of the devil is to devour, a graphic depiction of his desire to annihilate the Christian."[8] That's the bad news, but the good news is that Scripture speaks pointedly to Satan's strategy. The earliest Christians not only understood they had an enemy but they also knew their enemy's playbook.

First, Peter says, "Stay alert!" On this side of heaven, you have to operate on the assumption that Satan is always working, and because he is working, you have to be watching. Satan doesn't take days off, so neither can you. The security of your interior life requires a vigilance that rules out spiritual "cheat days" or anything less than our full-on pursuit of all that God has for us. Often what people fail to realize is that Satan has had the opportunity to observe humans for millennia, and because of this, he knows the vulnerabilities of your heart far better than you do. He is in many ways like the coach of a rival football team constantly watching your game film. He knows when you are most likely to falter. He has studied your mess-ups, mistakes, and missed opportunities. When God asks Satan where he has been at the beginning of the book of Job, notice his answer: "The LORD said to Satan, 'Where have you come from?' Satan answered the LORD, 'From roaming throughout the earth, going back and forth on it.'"[9] And he never stops looking. So how do you know when he is most likely to attack?

Second, much like a thief, the devil is an opportunist. Peter says the devil "prowls . . . looking." Satan doesn't know the future, and Satan cannot read your mind. The Creator God revealed in Scripture is described as omnipotent (all-powerful), omnipresent (everywhere simultaneously), and omniscient (all-knowing). Satan possesses none of those "omnis." But he is on the prowl. He is looking for opportunities to exploit your areas of weakness. He is patient. He is willing to wait for the right moment. He watches financial pressure build until the optimal opening to introduce a less-than-honest way for you to get ahead at the expense of someone else. He watches the tension build between you and someone you love until the optimal opening to instigate conflict. He watches your entertainment choices when you are worn down, looking for the optimal opening to put something in front of you that crosses the line of what you know you should be looking at or thinking about. This is how temptation works. Billy Sunday says, "Temptation is the devil looking through the keyhole."[10] He can't create these opportunities, he can only look for them, so Peter says you have to "stay alert."

Third, Satan and sin have the same endgame. Their goal is not to wound. Their goal is to destroy. Peter says Satan is "looking for someone to devour." You might not know any Greek, but the word translated "devour" in 1 Peter 5:8 is a fun one to learn. It's pronounced *kata-peeno*. It means "to swallow," and can even be translated "to disappear underground."[11] It's the same word that is used for Jonah being swallowed by the whale in the Greek translation of the Old Testament. When we hear those definitions, the word picture that seems to best sum up this term in our minds is the sarlacc pit that Jabba the Hutt tries to drop Luke Skywalker into in *Return of the Jedi* (spoiler alert: it doesn't work, because Luke is not only a Jedi but also a gold-medal-level gymnast). The *Star Wars Encyclopedia* describes the sarlacc as an "omnivorous, multi-tentacled creature with needle-sharp teeth."[12] When Peter uses the word "devour," he wants you to understand that Satan wants you to disappear. His goal is to swallow you and everything you care about, and he loves to start with the heart. In fact, you can watch this play out to tragic effect in the lives of two of the first Christians, Ananias and Sapphira. They are caught in a lie told to make themselves look good, but Peter identifies the root of the problem when he says, "Ananias, why have you let Satan fill your heart?"[13] And the sad conclusion of their story dramatically illustrates how Satan devours.

The devil is going to center his attack where he can do the most damage, so his target will always be the heart. The question is: How do you set a double guard?

A Double Guard Against the Devil

Our families love dogs, and both of us currently have a big outdoor dog. But their size is about where the similarities end. David has a Siberian husky named Denali. She is friendly but alert. She is protective of the children. She is constantly scanning the wooded perimeter of the yard. And every few weeks she brings her latest kill to the driveway or the patio for display. One of her ears is even ripped, a prominent war wound that demonstrates her willingness to fight. Brandon has a goldendoodle named Gus. He is friendly but aloof. He goes where the wind blows. He has boundless, undirected energy. Life is his playground, and he loves to play. Gus lives unencumbered by the need to guard. After all, Gus is a lover, not a fighter. That is a delightful disposition for a dog, but it is a destructive disposition for a heart.

An unguarded heart is a careless heart, and that carelessness creates the ideal conditions for Satan's attack. Yet, setting a double guard against the devil is not complicated, it just takes intentionality and resolve.

The security of the heart starts with sounding the alarm. Peter says, "Resist him."[14] Remember, Satan may be a roaring lion, but New Testament scholar Tom Schreiner writes, "The roaring of the devil is the crazed anger of a defeated enemy, and if they do not fear his ferocious bark, they will never be consumed by his bite."[15] In other words, this is a battle you can win. But it's how you resist the devil that makes all the difference. Think about how the apostle Paul filled out this call to resistance against Satan in writing to the young church he had planted in Ephesus:

> Finally, be strong in the Lord and in his mighty power. Put on the full armor of God, so that you can take your stand against the devil's schemes. For our struggle is not against flesh and blood, but against the rulers, against the authorities, against the powers of this dark world and against the spiritual forces of evil in the heavenly realms. Therefore put on the full armor of God, so that when the day of evil comes, you may be able to stand your ground, and after you have done everything, to stand.[16]

The double guard that allows you to resist the devil starts with strength. The old adage "the best defense is a good offense" is often attributed to a football coach (New England Patriots fans would no doubt insist it was Bill Belichick), but its roots go all the way back to George Washington. But even if Washington is the one who originally voiced a version of these words, he was articulating a principle of spiritual warfare established by God. A double guard doesn't start with thinking about what the enemy is doing and responding to him; it has to be established long before the enemy shows up. Knowing what the devil is doing will mean next to nothing if you aren't personally prepared to handle his attack. Knowing what the devil is doing is also useless unless you know your own heart well enough to preemptively prepare for the battles Satan is bringing your way. Think about temptation for a moment. Too many of us view temptation as something we stumble into, not recognizing that there are stages in our response to temptation, and when we pay attention to what's happening in us and around us, we can be very effective at stopping temptation in its tracks. In fact, John Flavel provides one of the most helpful step-by-step analyses of the way that temptation works in a person's heart. As you read this, think about how this plays out in your own life. Now, I am warning you, some of his phrasing is going to sound a bit funny (dare I say antiquated), because he wrote this over 350 years ago. But it is solid gold.

> It is the watchful heart that discovers and suppresses the temptation before it comes to its strength. . . . There is the irritation of the object (some temptation worthy of

your attention), or that power it has to provoke our corrupt nature; which is either done by the real presence of
the object, or by speculation when the object (though
absent) is held out by the imagination before the soul.
Then follows the motion of the appetite, which is pro-
voked by the fancy representing it as a sensual good. Then
there is a consultation in the mind about the best means
of accomplishing it. Next follows the election, or choice
of the will. And last, the desire, or full engagement of
the will to it. All this may be done in a few minutes, for
the debates of the soul are quick and soon ended: when
it comes thus far, the heart is won, Satan has entered
victoriously and displayed his colors upon the walls of
that royal fort; but, had the heart been well guarded at
first, it had never come to this—the temptation had been
stopped in the first or second act. And indeed there it is
stopped easily; for it is in the motion of a soul tempted to
sin, as in the motion of a stone falling from the brow of a
hill—it is easily stopped at first, but when once it is set in
motion "it acquires strength by descending." *Therefore it
is the greatest wisdom to observe the first motions of the
heart.* (Emphasis added, because you cannot miss this!)[17]

This is an incredible insight for any man battling temptation, especially if you can't figure out how to get the
upper hand over sin that you just keep repeating. Flavel is
saying that the genesis point of every temptation is something or someone catching your eye or a thought passing
through your mind. Then, instead of looking away or intentionally rejecting and replacing the thought, you begin
to toy with the idea of how good it would feel (regardless
of what "it" is). Next you are figuring out how to get away

with it. Now comes the moment of decision, followed by giving in. All of this only takes a matter of minutes or even seconds, but the whole process would have come to a screeching halt if you had recognized what was happening right from the start.

If you just breezed through that, read it again. Read it until you internalize it. Those words speak directly to why you are first called to "be strong in the Lord and in his mighty power,"[18] and it's also why in Ephesians 3 Paul tells his readers that he is praying that they will "be strengthened with power through his Spirit in your inner being."[19] If you are not strong, then there is no way you are going to be ready to stop temptation or any other attack before it gets the upper hand in your life. If you aren't spiritually strong, then your ability to accurately assess what Flavel calls "the first motions of the heart" will be greatly diminished.

Maybe this is a good place to ask yourself a few honest questions: How strong are you? (We're not asking about your muscle mass or your body fat percentage. We are talking spiritually. This is a question about inner strength.) Be candid about where you really are on the journey toward a robust relationship with God. Are you stronger than you have ever been before? And if not, why not? On a scale of 1–10, how prepared are you for the enemy's attack? Answering these questions is essential if you are going to be ready to resist the heist from hell. But knowing that you need to be strong and that you need to be ready is not the same as being strong and being ready, so now we need to look at how you own the responsibility to resist.

After all, the Old Testament prophet Jeremiah said no one can really know the heart, so having a guarded heart without the help of the Holy Spirit is impossible. Trying to fortify the most important part of who you are in your own strength is a fool's errand. The good news is that because the Holy Spirit lives inside of you, you already have the person who knows you best ready, willing, and able to help you protect what matters most. You can pray, "Holy Spirit, reveal to me places where I need to better guard my heart." He will do it, but what you have to understand is that though the Holy Spirit is ready to help you, He is not going to do everything for you. He will resource you to resist the assault of the enemy, but you have to be strong in the Lord to have a well-guarded heart. Being strong in the Lord is not just spiritual jargon for being a super-Christian. It is the language the New Testament uses for people who are engaged in the fight against darkness and have armed themselves for the conflict with the perfectly suited weaponry that God provides.

"Therefore put on the full armor of God."[20] We think of armor as something you wear on a limited basis. You only put it on as needed. But that is not the mentality of the apostle Paul. He has a wartime mentality; he means for every one of us to live in our armor. A double-guarded heart—consequently a well-guarded heart—requires it. In Ephesians 6, we get a detailed list of the armor we need to be wearing, and it starts with the belt of truth. In first-century warfare, the belt was vital because it held everything else in place and kept the warrior from getting tangled up in his own clothing and equipment. It anchored the rest of the soldier's gear. Truth functions the same way in the life of faith. What truth are we talking about here? This is primarily the truth of God's Word, which finds its epicenter in the message of the gospel. If your life is not anchored with that, you will constantly be tripping over yourself instead of triumphing in battle. A double-guarded heart also needs something that is specifically designed to cover the heart. That's why the next piece listed is "the breastplate of righteousness."[21] This plate protected the soldier's vital organs in the same way righteousness shields the core of your inner life. But this righteousness is not your righteous acts; it is something that is given to you—the righteousness of God in Christ that you have to receive as a gift. Here is Paul's description of what that means:

> But whatever were gains to me I now consider loss for the sake of Christ. What is more, I consider everything a loss because of the surpassing worth of knowing Christ Jesus my Lord, for whose sake I have lost all things. I consider them garbage, that I may gain Christ and be found in him, not having a righteousness of my own that comes from the law, but that which is through faith in Christ—the righteousness that comes from God on the basis of faith.[22]

The source of this righteousness is not you, but you do have a God-assignment and the God-ability to walk in that righteousness.[23] With this armor comes the power to avoid falling prey to the devil's constant assault of shame and condemnation. With it, you reject the lie that you have to earn right standing with God. You put on the breastplate because it surrounds you and strengthens you in a way your own efforts never could.

Now it's time to get some footwear, specifically having "your feet fitted with the readiness that comes from the gospel of peace."[24] In reading this verse, it's fair to wonder how "the gospel of peace" makes you ready and what that has to do with your feet. Kent Hughes writes, "The image Paul has in mind comes from the Roman soldier's war boot, the *caliga* or half-boot which the legionnaire regularly wore while on duty. It was an open-toed leather boot with a heavily-nail-studded sole that was tied to the ankles and shins with straps. These were not shoes for running—for example, fleeing or pursuing an enemy."[25] These were battle cleats. They were designed to help you keep the ground you had taken. They made the soldiers sure-footed so they could not be pushed back, slip, or slide. God gives you a peace that is the footing of the Christian life. Without peace with God and the peace of God resting on you, the devil will inevitably be able to push you around.

Now it's time to pick up a weapon. If you are like most people, the first weapon you are grabbing is something sharp, but the first thing Scripture tells us to grab is the shield, namely the shield of faith. The fact is that Satan intends to unleash as much of his arsenal against you as possible. There is no question he will attack anything and everything that he feels might get him close to his prime target—your faith. He wants to burn your faith to the ground, so if that means attacking your health, your marriage, your finances, your relationships, your family, or anything else, he will do it. He will fire the arrows of hell at anything he thinks has your heart. And this is why the shield of faith is so critical: it not only has the capability of blocking his assault, it also can "extinguish" his flaming arrows. Part of Paul's point here is that if you are going to use anything to shield your life, it better be faith. People try to use all sorts of substitutes as safeguards, but none of them are effective at extinguishing the enemy's weaponry—only faith is.

Finally, we get our last war implements—the helmet and the sword. We grew up skateboarding. Our dad built us ramps. Our parents bought us a rail to grind on. We skated every area of the church parking lot. We worked on our ollies and unsuccessfully practiced our sad versions of kickflips. We were so cool (well, we thought we were). But the first piece of equipment our parents acquired for us was helmets. Strange as it may sound, they never had to talk us into wearing them. Why? Because they were confidence builders. Having a helmet allowed for one less cause for concern. In a much greater way, the helmet of salvation has the same effect. When you go into battle with this helmet, you know that no matter what happens to you or comes at you, you have been saved by God's grace and are part of His family. None of that is ever in question. But the helmet is paired with the sword of the Spirit. If you have been paying attention, then you have noticed that every piece of armor up to this point has been for defense. The pieces we have already covered may help you hold ground, but you need a sword to take ground. When you are armed with "the sword of the Spirit, which is the word of God," you are ready to conquer your enemy.[26] This is why the New Testament writer John says, "I write to you, young men, because you are strong, and the word of God lives in you, and you have overcome the evil one."[27]

With all of this language about the enemy's continual assault on the lives of men, we are aware that you may be reading this wondering why your life doesn't feel like the frontlines. The answers to that question vary. It could be that God has allowed you a season of rest that is meant to replenish strength. If that's the case, make it count. It could also be that you haven't thought of the challenges you are facing as a part of the enemy's attack because you have only been looking at things from a natural vantage point instead of recognizing the supernatural realities of life. Or—and this one might hurt a little—maybe you just aren't much of a threat. If you don't live with any urgency to advance the kingdom of God and push back darkness, then it could be that Satan views your life as not worth his time. Regardless, it's time to wake up! A double guard against the devil cannot be passive. Your strategy cannot be to find a bunker to hide in. That's not the life of faith. That's not the calling of a Christian. That's not how you see Satan stopped. And here's the promise. There is victory on the other side of your resistance. You don't have to allow your heart to fall prey to the enemy. You can deny the devil the access to your heart that you may have given him in the past. You can take up armor that will break the cycle. It will be a battle. There will be a fight. But if you resist, his heist will fail, and he will flee:

Resist the devil, and he will flee from you.[28]

07

The Jaws of Life (and Death)

Words kill, words give life; they're either
poison or fruit—you choose.
Proverbs 18:21 MSG

Don't speak unless you can improve on the silence.
Spanish proverb

The concern was speed, not caution, as stock cars ripped around the Indianapolis Motor Speedway one day in May 1961. The adrenaline fueled by acceleration quickly shifted to panic as one of the cars flipped, reducing it to a pile of mangled metal.[1] The crowd stared in horror as first responders rushed to the devastating scene to rescue the driver trapped inside the crumpled vehicle.

Seconds turned into minutes, and minutes turned into an entire hour as emergency workers tediously labored to free the racer from the wreckage. The feeling of helplessness that permeated the horrific scene gave way to a strange spark of inspiration for one person in the crowd.[2] A young inventor named George Hurst was watching the tedious tragedy unfold, and though rescuers would eventually save the driver, the slow minutes of waiting would change the rest of George's life. He left the speedway with a determination that would transform the future of emergency response.[3]

Eighth grade was as far as George made it in school before dropping out to join the navy. But when an injury abruptly ended his stint in the armed forces, he got a garage, which would turn out to be the environment best suited for his inventive mind.[4] George had not only mechanical know-how but the desire to create. After witnessing the accident, he was on a mission to design something that would give rescuers the strength to snatch people from the jaws of death. Armed with his love for cars and a burning desire to innovate, George had used his expertise in the past to make cars faster, but now his passion became to make rescues quicker.

His first prototype was bulky and cumbersome—think a 350-pound set of hydraulic pliers.[5] The creation was much too heavy and difficult to maneuver for death-defying rescues.[6] Yet George refused to give up. For a decade, he worked to refine his design before he unveiled it to the world in 1971. The final product was powerful, maneuverable, and capable, with 120,000 pounds of cutting force—enough to cut through a six-inch steel beam like butter.[7] This awe-inspiring invention came to be known as the Jaws of Life and has saved countless lives, changing the course of automotive history.

Things That Could Kill You

Isn't it wild how what has the power to kill also has the power to comfort? A fire can keep you warm, or it can burn you alive. You can ride the waves, or the waves can capsize your boat. In the apocalyptic imagination of Revelation, Jesus Himself, the sacrificial "Lamb of God,"[8] is also revealed as the "Lion of the tribe of Judah"—and it is an image meant to inspire comfort and not fear among the people of God.[9]

Lions are not just powerful; they are the very definition of power. No wonder we are always drawn to them in art, mythology, and literature—their primal power stalks our imagination. They are majestic, but there is a boyish part of us that is both inspired and terrified knowing those teeth could tear apart virtually anything or anyone. Like storms, like fire, like the sea, lions fall under the *Jeopardy* category of "things that are awesome but could also kill you for $800, Alex."

But you already know about this kind of power, don't you? You don't have to live in a penthouse or own a private jet to know about power. I bet you know what it's like to have an early crush say something savage that tore you apart in a way you can still remember years later. I bet you know what it's like to have someone you admire and respect pay you a compliment that makes you feel like you could never feel bad about yourself again. I bet you know what it's like to say something to someone you love that was so potent and full of life, you could almost see their heart inflate and expand in front of you. I bet you know what it's like to say something to someone you love in a moment of anger that was so reckless, so unintentionally cruel, that you could watch the carnage spread over them in real time.

We have all felt the sting of a sarcastic remark that was meant to wound or a well-placed verbal sucker punch that induced a laugh at our expense. Usually, the most hurtful and memorable verbal attacks come from the people closest to us—the comments of a family member or friend that we just can't seem to forget. The teeth of the remarks went deep, and we have never fully healed. All of us know what it's like to be assaulted by another person's words.

But words also have the capacity to heal, to mend, to soothe, to protect. Words have an endless capacity for good. Like George Hurst, put yourself on a mission to impact the lives of people around you for good through the powerful tool of your words. As the writer of Proverbs says, "Words kill, words give life; they're either poison or fruit—you choose."[10] This is just another way of articulating the biblical truth that our words possess the power of life and death. Our words are not just words; they shape our reality and the reality of those around us. Jesus said they are also the most honest and accurate assessment of what is present inside of us.[11] The implications are nothing short of shocking. But the sad truth is, just like lions, our words are more readily associated with death than with life.

Whether you feel powerful or powerless right now, you already know about power. Intuitively, you know that your mouth was made for blessing. You know because you have experienced that power in words that you have received and words you have delivered. Like the God who created us in His image, who blessed everything that He made ("It was very good!"), we carry the same life-giving, world-building power within our tongues.

Tongues in Satan's Service

Words can burn. That doesn't sound exaggerated if you've ever had any words inside of you that were on fire—burning in the late-night hours, engulfing your imagination, taking over your sleeping and waking hours. Have you ever, in anger and anxiety, lain awake rehearsing conversations or strategically planning what you would say for a future interaction? Burning on the inside. It's easier to talk about how this happens to us. It's less comfortable to talk about how our words have affected others—about the times we were the ones who lit the fuse. It's easier to talk about the times we have felt victimized than the times our words have actually made victims of people we ostensibly care about.

Since we are talking about fires that burn, about words that burn with seemingly unending flames of destruction, it seems like a good time to bring up Satan. Doesn't it feel like a left turn to bring up Satan in most any conversation? There's a wild moment in the Gospels when Jesus is talking to His friends, and Peter says something that gets this response from Jesus: "Get behind me, Satan!"[12] I don't know what Peter's first thought was, but I'm pretty sure it was not, "That's definitely what I was expecting you to say." Maybe talk of Satan in most conversations feels like a hard turn. But the moment this happens is instructive. Jesus obviously wasn't vindictive, and He clearly wasn't telling Peter that he was literally Satan or trying to send him to therapy for thirty years. Cut to scene: "Who hurt you?" the therapist asks from an old leather chair. "Well, you see, Doc, it was Jesus." "Jesus? Oh, you know that He loves you. I'm sure He didn't mean it." "Yeah, but see, He actually called me Satan." (Therapist scribbles furiously.)

It's a funny image, but we know that Jesus really wasn't saying that Peter somehow morphed into a devil, like something out of a horror movie. What He was saying is Peter flippantly said something that would have subverted Jesus's whole salvation agenda had He taken it seriously, so it was something more like, "Satan has entered the chat." Peter wasn't a literal devil, but he was saying something the actual devil would say in physical form if he could. Like when we say something edifying or beautiful, there is a real way that the power and goodness of God is somehow manifested in our words, but it works in the opposite direction too. We can become unintentional messengers of the evil one.

If you are not up on your '70s glam metal, the carnival act rock band KISS famously was thought to be an acronym for "Knights in Satan's Service." The singer Gene Simmons has denied this, but the idea stuck. While we don't necessarily think "Tongues in Satan's Service" will be a future find in vintage T-shirt shops, it does get the job done! We don't tend to think of ourselves as mouthpieces for Satan; in fact, we prefer to see ourselves in the opposite light. This is why this passage in James 3 is so troubling:

> If we put bits into the mouths of horses so that they obey us, we guide their whole bodies as well. Look at the ships also: though they are so large and are driven by strong winds, they are guided by a very small rudder wherever the will of the pilot directs. So also the tongue is a small member, yet it boasts of great things. How great a forest is set ablaze by such a small fire! And the tongue is a fire, a world of unrighteousness. The tongue is set among our members, staining the whole body, setting on fire the entire course of life, and set on fire by hell.[13]

The third chapter of James deals with our words, but the bigger point he is making is that what comes out of our mouths directly impacts the direction of our lives. While we expect the Bible to have lots to say about our words, the forcefulness of James's imagery is jolting.

With dynamic metaphors, the author reveals the might our words possess. His first two images—a bit in a horse's mouth and the rudder on a massive ship—allude to the tongue's exacting control over a person, which can dramatically influence the direction of their life. While these images are decidedly neutral, the writer's third image is unquestionably negative. "How great a forest is set ablaze by such a small fire!" he exclaims.[14] Just like a forest fire, the tongue can burn up a life as its words spread rapidly, leaving little hope of reversing or containing the devastation that follows in their wake.

In verse 6, James takes it a step further to say that the tongue actually *is* a fire. There is real-world destruction in its words, and its ruin is easy to see. We glimpse it in the pained laugh of someone made the butt of a snarky joke, in the embarrassment of a child publicly berated by a parent, in the flushed face of a woman whose inadequacies are routinely paraded by her spouse—each scenario smells eerily of smoke. James goes on to say that with these words we become the mouthpiece of hell, because the tongue's fire is fueled by hell itself.

Our hellish words "[stain] the whole body."[15] They penetrate deeply, resembling the "sword thrusts" described in Proverbs 12.[16] The internal damage they inflict twinges unexpressed long after the conversation ends, setting aflame "the entire course of life."[17] James borrowed this phrase from first-century pagan religious language: it refers to the unending cycle of reincarnation. The implication is that the words we say assume a life of their own. They keep coming back to burn up what had almost healed.

What James says next is devastating. If the tongue is a fire, it is a fire you cannot prevent: "No human being can tame the tongue."[18]

So, what do we do? What can we do? The early church father Augustine offered hope when he wrote in his book *On Nature and Grace*, "For he does not say, 'No one can tame the tongue,' but 'no man,' so that, when it is tamed, we may admit that it was done by the mercy of God, the assistance of God, the grace of God."[19] It isn't a matter of mustering up enough self-discipline—watching our language or shutting our mouths, as we've all likely been admonished to do. Taming the tongue can only be done by the enabling grace of God.

Going Deeper

To get to the root of this, we must go deeper. Specifically, we have to drop down from our heads to our chest cavity, because that's where the action (and the trouble) really is. The way we think about our words is often superficial, as if what happens above the surface matters more than what happens beneath the surface. Spoiler alert: it doesn't.

Words come from deep places, and they shape deep places within us. James continues: "With [our tongue] we bless our Lord and Father, and with it we curse people who are made in the likeness of God."[20] That last phrase calls to mind some of the very first words of Scripture: "Let us make man in our image, after our likeness."[21] This connection to creation shows this passage is about more than the tongue—it's about our identity.

Words ground our identity. What we say and what others say about us—whether positive or negative—shapes who we are, and how we see ourselves. We can't divorce ourselves from what comes out of our mouths. Jesus articulates this reality: "It is not what goes into the mouth that defiles a person, but what comes out of the mouth; this defiles a person. . . . What comes out of the mouth proceeds from the heart."[22] This is why words are not just about the tongue: they are directly connected to who we are—to our identity—and they are intimately connected to the core of our being.

In other words, we can wash our mouths out with soap all we want, but the issue isn't really the mouth but the heart. This is the point James reinforces repeatedly:

Does a salt spring produce fresh water? Nope.
Do olives grow on a fig tree? Nope.
Do figs grow on a grapevine? Nope.[23]

Why? Because producing those things is contrary to their identity.

The more clearly you grasp your identity in Christ, the more clearly you will see the destructive power of the tongue diminished as your words begin to align with your true self. Because what's coming out of your mouth is first coming out of your heart. So yes, Satan might use you as a megaphone, but the root of the problem is at your core and, once again, the issue is not that your heart is corrupted—it's that it's being co-opted. It's being used as a vessel for the wrong things, and your words are just the evidence of a much bigger problem.

Where Words Come From

Only God creates out of nothing. Contrary to what we often say about our words, they actually do come from somewhere—and they have weight and meaning, even if their weight and meaning have not been carefully considered. Our words are not arbitrary accidents like meteors that fall from the sky unexpectedly onto the people around us. They are extensions of us and expressions of us, expressions of things that are happening within the depths.

Ever the master teacher, Jesus describes this with shattering precision: "For out of the abundance of the heart the mouth speaks. The good person out of his good treasure brings forth good, and the evil person out of his evil treasure brings forth evil."[24] This verse makes it impossible to say dumb things like, "I didn't mean what I said," or "I am sorry you felt like what I said was insensitive." Warning: that's not a real apology. Doing that in marriage is like poking a grizzly bear. The problem with these statements is that they are wrong and unbiblical. They are unmanly and ungodly. Truth be told, you said what you said, and you need to own that. Why? It came from your heart. Oh, it might have flowed from a hard heart or a hurt heart or a poisoned, bitter heart, but it came from *your* heart. Own that.

Pause here and think about this. If you don't want to say dumb or hurtful things that you'll regret, the key is not only getting better at guarding your mouth but installing a better security system on your heart. It feels like someone is thinking as they are reading this, "Well, what they are doing is so wrong, and it's not my fault if I speak from that hurt. It's honest." You are wrong. True, you are not a robot and you have feelings, but what you do with those feelings is a choice. God gave you the ability to take responsibility and create the environment around you. This doesn't mean you control people, but it does mean you at the very least control you. Your new heart makes that possible, and with that you can be or, should we say, you *are called to be* lionhearted and a leader. Leaders can't help what other people do but they can take responsibility for what happens on the inside.

We are not talking about passing thoughts. We are talking about swirling thoughts. If you have ever been around a dead animal or roadkill, then you know it doesn't take long for vultures to begin to circle. These birds with impressive wingspans aren't flapping their wings over and over again to fly. They get lift from columns of heat rising from the sunbaked ground called thermals. This whole scene is a picture of your thought life if you are given to hard and hurtful statements.

Something died in your life. A disappointment happened. A hurtful situation occurred. Your dad, stepmom, wife, boss, best friend, or girlfriend said or did something, and it stung badly. Maybe it wasn't even a onetime thing. It happened over and over again. Maybe they didn't even know they did it or maybe they did, but something in your heart died. You drew a bitter conclusion: "They don't care" or "They're a full-blown jerk" or "They are all about themselves" or "They don't love me." Death has happened. Then, like vultures, the thoughts start to swirl in your heart. When these thoughts start circling in your head, usually some choice four-letter words are attached. It begins with a single thought, but then they start to come in abundance. Based on the number of thoughts you are having, there is no way they could last or stay in the air without lift, but like a thermal you feed them, giving them lift by your emotions and anger. More come, and now there is a scene of death with only scavengers ready to pick apart the rotting corpse. This is how dark things can get.

If you relate, then you are in real danger because you have an abundance of bad stuff on the inside—TNT of the soul. If you have not exploded yet, you will . . . if you don't dismantle this situation, fast. If reading the description above causes emotions and thoughts to stir up on the inside, that is the Holy Spirit. He is telling you that you need to do something about the abundance of toxic thoughts and feelings on the inside. These are going to lead to words, if they haven't already, and those words are going to frame your reality—and you are not going to like it. Our words have unimaginable power to both create and destroy. We won't understand just how crucial this interior work of the Holy Spirit really is until we grasp something of the inherent power of our words.

Your Words Can Stop a Storm

If you are human, then at some point you have probably found yourself mindlessly watching hydraulic press videos on YouTube. What? You haven't seen those? Then let us digress for the uninitiated. These world-class pieces of visual entertainment show the destruction a hydraulic press inflicts by crushing objects, from a bowling ball, to Legos, to a watermelon, to pretty much anything, you name it. It's mind-numbing and entertaining, and it's wild to think there are animal species that can inflict similarly terrifying destruction with their bite. Lions have a bite strength of 650 psi, which, when combined with their two-inch fangs, creates a devastatingly lethal combination. We usually think of that and shudder at the thought of our neck being snapped in one bite—but their primary purpose is usually not killing humans. It's deadly for their prey, but a blessing for the lions. Their superstrong jaws are what keep them alive.

Your mouth can be similar: deadly when your heart is in the wrong place, but a blessing when your heart is in the right place. Your mouth is like the jaws of a lion, and while we don't recommend trying to chew anything that would require a 650-psi bite strength, we do want you to understand the power of what you have.

Throughout the Bible we are given examples and teachings concerning the authority God has given us over the world around us through our words. Jesus said, "If you have faith . . . you can say to this mountain, 'Go, throw yourself into the sea,' and it will be done."[25] Maybe you have allowed the contemporary church to build so many analogies around Scriptures like this that it is difficult for you to really apply or believe it. Jesus was saying you can tell an inanimate object without a soul to obey you and it will obey. Another hang-up people have on this is they are afraid it leans into witchcraft. But witchcraft, like anything else that is demonic, is just imitating the real thing and borrowing authority. The devil knows your words have power and therefore he creates whole spiritual paths and demonic religions to twist this truth. Back to your words: they have power biblically—Jesus cursed a fig tree using His words, healed people using His words, and stopped a storm using His words. Proverbs teaches, "The tongue has the power of life and death."[26] This doesn't mean you control God or can do whatever you want (so don't go down some pointless theological tangent). Take Scripture at face value: God made you in His image and He is the same God who said, "Let there be light," and light happened.[27] Your words have power and authority.

That's why this chapter is called "The Jaws of Life (and Death)"—because if you don't recognize your authority and you have an abundance of bitterness in your heart, then, like a diseased lion, you are going to go around killing and destroying everything. Have you seen these people with pet lions? It's kind of cool . . . until the lion wakes up one day and decides their owner looks like a tasty snack. It's almost proverbial: "owner of exotic big cat killed suddenly for seemingly no reason." This isn't always because the lion was hungry; it could just be playing rough with its nonlion owner. Again, lions are powerful apex predators, so if they want to inflict damage, they have the authority to do so. Remember, Proverbs says, "Words kill, words give life; they're either poison or fruit—you choose."[28] You have that kind of authority with your mouth, and when you let stuff into your heart that seems small—but then the vultures start to circle—you can inflict major damage.

Maybe you are in the wake of a deadly-words moment as you read this book—where the authority and weight of your words are all too real right now. That's a heavy place to be. If that is you and you are not sure how to pick up the pieces from the nuclear bomb you detonated, don't despair. The same God who made your mouth with authority, who formed the universe with a word, that same God can lift you out of your current situation . . . but He will first deal with the inside. All through this book, we have been talking to you, sometimes pleading with you, to consider the state of your heart. Listen, nothing else matters as much as that. Everything flows out of it. EVERYTHING.

We have already unpacked the importance of the psalmist's prayer, "Search me, O God."[29] The truth is there are always things lurking under the surface that we may not see, but your words are one of the very best indicators of the actual state of your heart. People are incredibly fond of saying stupid things like, "You don't know my heart." The reason that's a dumb thing to say is because it's usually a defensive statement pulled out in the middle of an argument where our words have already betrayed us. In other words, you already said something unkind or mean or hateful, somebody called you on it, and now your comeback is that they don't know your heart—but they actually do. They know, because your words just gave them quality intel on what's really going on at the core of who you are. Maybe this isn't a moment to bow up and get defensive. Maybe this is the moment to recognize that you were more honest than you wanted to be, and your mouth just revealed some things happening on the inside that you aren't proud of—but now you have the opportunity to deal with them.

We mentioned the verse earlier that says, "The heart is deceitful above all things, and desperately wicked; who can know it?"[30] It's because of this truth that every chapter deals a bit with self-deception. We can't help you if you don't pull back some layers on the onion of self-deception. So, before we wrap up this chapter, let's go just a touch deeper.

Empowerment

The key to harnessing the power of our words goes back to what Jesus said about abundance: "Out of the abundance of the heart the mouth speaks."[31] You will never control the tongue if you don't change your heart.

You need to get everything out that even *smells* of an off attitude or spirit. You need to ask God to change the track that's playing over and over again in your mind. Abundance leads to empowerment. Honestly, you need the Holy Spirit to fill you up, and fill you up with the right things. "But I have tried that," you say. Then we would counter with, "Not adequately." The Holy Spirit is good, but He knows it doesn't really help you if He just changes you without you crying out to Him. When you half-heartedly pray, "God change my heart," while you are sitting on the toilet, it's nice (sarcasm added), but it will not cut it. It's when you pray and you feel like He is not hearing you, but you are desperate enough to push through in prayer into the heavens—that's when God does some of His best work. He is not trying to torture you, but you do need to cry out. Cry out to heaven. Say, "God, if you don't change my heart, I am destined to destroy. I am destined to be hard-hearted. I am destined to kill the good things you have given me and my God-given purpose." He will transform your heart. You will know it. You will sense Him like a flood. He will change your heart, and you will be empowered to change your words. You can't transform your own heart—only God can. Ask God for help. He will put things inside of you that you never thought were possible: a tenderness toward your wife that you couldn't come up with on your own, a respect for your boss you couldn't conjure up alone, a love for that person who hurt you.

You may have heard it said, "Don't give that person who hurt you free real estate in your heart," and that's good advice, but Jesus takes it a step further and says to really love them. When you find an abundance from the

Holy Spirit, you will start to use your lionhearted, God-given authority for good. You will be empowered to love and bring life-giving change to the desolate environments around you. Stop here and right now pray,

Jesus, let the words of my mouth and the things I think about be pleasing to You. I reject every hateful, bitter, angry, or cutting thought I have allowed to live in my heart. That ends today. Holy Spirit, please fill me with Your life and abundance. Thank You for loving me and caring enough about me to make me lionhearted. Amen.

08

The Eyes of a Lion

Look straight ahead, and fix your
eyes on what lies before you.
Proverbs 4:25 NLT

We desperately need seers
who can see through the mist.
A. W. Tozer

The plane loaded with 153 passengers was cruising at 36,000 feet, but air traffic control was getting no response. The flight was veering off course, but the only thing coming from the cockpit of the Airbus was panic-inducing stillness. A menu of nightmare scenarios began to float through safety officials' minds. Had the plane been hijacked? Was the crew dealing with a medical emergency? Could it be a mechanical failure?

Even other pilots tried to make contact with the drifting aircraft. But there had been no response from Flight 6723. The radio silence persisted.

Then all of a sudden, the pilots' voices came through loud and clear. They were off course, but everything was fine—they had both just woken up from a nap.

Yep, a nap.

The embarrassing truth was that thirty minutes into the Jakarta-bound flight, the captain had leaned over to his twenty-eight-year-old copilot—a newly minted father of twins—to ask if it was okay if he took a nap. The copilot had agreed, but soon this sleep-deprived dad closed his eyes as well and nodded off. Both pilots were sound asleep in the cockpit with no one paying attention to the instruments, the radio, or where the plane was going.[1]

This story probably does not help with your fear of flying. But it paints an appropriately terrifying picture of what happens when we allow our eyes to get off what is most important.

The Path Is Not a Problem

One of the joys of being a pastor is helping people process their questions, and as you may have noticed, human beings have lots of questions. We have Yelp to help us figure out who has the best meatball sub in a five-mile radius. We have NerdWallet to help us find the credit card that will give us the most points for each purchase. We have Rotten Tomatoes to help us assess our entertainment options. And of course, YouTube to answer our most pressing home improvement questions. And yet, something we have noticed is that many of the people who come to us with their spiritual questions are concerned about direction. They want to know that they are going the right way. They are worried about what's in front of them. They don't want to miss where they are supposed to be going. Those questions and concerns aren't wrong, but as the writer of Proverbs points out, they shouldn't be our primary concern. He says, "Look straight ahead, and fix your eyes on what lies before you."[2] In Hebrew, the word translated "straight ahead" is *lenokach*, which comes with the built-in assumption that the path ahead of you is straight.[3] As Old Testament scholar Duane Garrett points out, "The idea is that one should not be distracted from the way of wisdom."[4] So, the concern is not so much direction as it is distraction.

We live in a world filled with opportunities for distraction. You are probably fighting a bunch of distractions right now as you try to read this book. Many of these are just part of life.

The raindrops tapping against the window.

The rumble of the subway.

The passing thought about the wall you've been meaning to paint.

The project due next week at work.

Squirrel.

So. Many. Distractions.

But in addition to the distractions that are baked into life, there are all the other ones that we invite in. Aldous Huxley labeled this "man's almost infinite appetite for distraction."[5] And yes, most of those involve the small screen that fits in your pocket. Now, remember, Solomon wrote Proverbs in a pre-iPhone world. So, distractions are nothing new, but it's easier than ever to get our eyes off the path in front of us. In fact, as you read the word *iPhone*, you were probably tempted to make sure you hadn't missed anything in the sixty seconds since you checked it last. It's fair to say that our twenty-first-century default is to live in a constant state of distraction. One study found that the average person touches their phone 2,617 times a day.[6] Researchers tell us that Americans spend an average of four hours and twenty-five minutes on their phone every day in addition to the time we spend watching TV.[7] This is not to say that our phones are the problem, but our propensity to make this our distraction of choice is accelerated by the dopamine hit our brain gets every time we look at that pocket-size screen. That said, we aren't victims. We are enablers, again and again giving our time and attention to what doesn't matter. We are willing slaves to the buzz alerting us that a friend updated their profile picture. We repeatedly choose to cultivate an insatiable appetite for the trivial. Scrolling. Scrolling. Scrolling. As Neil Postman writes with prophetic edge in his 1985 treatise *Amusing Ourselves to Death*, "People will come to adore the technologies that undo their capacities to think."[8] This is death by distraction.

Never Enough

"No matter how much we see, we are never satisfied."[9] Those words were written by the same guy who penned

Proverbs. What he means is people are never like, "I hate seeing. I think I have seen enough. I would be fine if I never saw anything ever again." No, you NEVER feel you have seen enough beauty, color, light. Your eyes are hungry. They always want more, and this insatiable desire your eyes have for more makes it easy to get off track. You would think that something as simple as a distracted glance would NOT be the action that changes your life for the good or the bad. We look at all sorts of things throughout our day. The fact is, while it may seem like your attention is locked in, while reading this chapter you are actually moving in and out of focus up to four times per second. Some people call it squirrel brain, and you may not think you have it but (sorry) you do. This is how your brain is wired to survive, and if you are the kind of person who likes to text while walking, it has probably saved your life more times than you realize.[10] However, it's not so great when you don't want to be distracted or are tempted to look at something that you shouldn't. Add to that a hulk-strength hardwired love for pleasure and that's where problems really happen.

You not only love seeing, you love pleasure. Everyone does. You might be the kind of tough guy who runs weekly marathons and embraces arctic cold plunges, but no matter how macho you are, you still love to feel good. You like sex, food, sleep, and anything else that produces a dopamine hit, probably in that order. And pleasure compounds our distraction tendency. Combine our innate love for seeing with our strong desire for pleasure, and a potentially lethal vortex of carnal craving has been born. A never-ending appetite combined with a serious desire.

This is where addiction is conceived and why millions if not billions of men can't stop looking at porn. Even if they don't think it's good for them or their relationships. And it all started with a look.

Though there are certainly biological ramifications to a steady diet of distraction, the greatest threat is its effect on your heart. Jesus said, "The eye is the lamp of the body. If your eyes are healthy, your whole body will be full of light. But if your eyes are unhealthy, your whole body will be full of darkness. If then the light within you is darkness, how great is that darkness!"[11] This is the reason that right after Solomon speaks directly to guarding our hearts in Proverbs 4:23, he targets our eyes. What you look at can't help but impact the health of your inner life, and our physical bodies provide an insightful correlation to this reality. Doctors have noted that the eyes are the first place you can observe signs of heart disease.[12] The physical mirrors the spiritual. Charles Spurgeon is right on target when he says, "It is the tendency of things that are gazed at to get through the eyes into the mind and the heart."[13] And don't miss that in Proverbs Solomon doesn't say the problem with not looking straight ahead only comes from viewing things that are overtly sinful, but it's looking at anything that's not the direction you are going.

Both of us are snowboarders, which means we've fallen down a lot. It comes with the territory. But after you learn to stay upright, the next hurdle is trying to figure out how to steer. This is especially critical when the people surrounding you on the mountain seem to be just as good or better at falling than you are. Make no mistake, falling is an art form. We have been part of some major pileups in the powder. We have also caused a few. The ability to avoid those is a major win. The tendency of most newly minted snowboarders is to watch their board or the people flying by them. The bad news is that strategy not only doesn't get you where you want to go, it inevitably leads to some epic wipeouts. Don't look down, and don't look around! As a wise snowboard instructor once said, "Keep your eyes on the prize." In other words, look where you want to go. But we can promise you that in snowboarding and in life that kind of focus does not happen by accident. The problem is that distractions come easily. Focus is hard. This is why to keep your eyes on where you are going, you have to pre-decide.

Pre-Deciding to Filter Your Focus

You can pre-decide to filter out what you know is not going to help you. As pastor Adrian Rogers says, "How you think governs what you see."[14] His point is that you don't have to give your focus to whatever comes across your field of vision. You have the ability and responsibility to set a filter for your focus. If you wait until the moment your eyes see something, some images are just too powerful to look away from if you haven't made the decision to beforehand.

There is no shortage of things to look at, and our tendency is to let life happen to us. We move from moment to moment allowing whatever we happen upon to potentially become the next thing we give our attention to. The problem is that much of what catches our eye during a given day doesn't deserve a second look, but if we haven't made a conscious pre-decision to filter our focus, we end up allowing our eyes to lead us instead of our convictions.

The Bible is filled with pre-deciding statements that specifically relate to what you choose to look at. Once again, King David, who wrote most of the Psalms, is incredibly helpful. Listen to his pre-decision statement about his eyes in Psalm 101:3: "I will not set before my eyes anything that is worthless" (ESV). This is a powerful statement about the future of his focus. He has determined to exclude certain things from his field of vision. The Hebrew word translated as "worthless" is made up of two words. It's a combination of the word *without* and the word *profit*. The term literally means "the quality of being useless, good for nothing."[15] So the litmus test is, Does it profit your soul? This is the generic filter that David pre-decided would guide what he allowed his eyes to look at, but most of us need to get specific about things that we aren't going to let our eyes look at. Another lionhearted man from the pages of Scripture, Job, said, "I made a covenant with my eyes not to look with lust at a young woman."[16] This is a pact that every man needs to make, but it's also an example of someone who is done with a haphazard approach to living and looking.

Job was clearly a man who understood the dominos that fall when your eyes wander. You will always live in the direction that you look. The lustful glance isn't just about the look, it's about the direction of your life and the legacy you are leaving. It's about devaluing a person made in the image of God by turning them into an object for your personal gratification. It's about dishonoring the

Creator because that's God's daughter. It's about cheapening God's gift of sex that was created to be enjoyed and treasured in the sacred context of marriage. It's about setting a trajectory for your sons and grandsons that paves the way toward generational enslavement to fantasy, lust, porn, masturbation, and all the garbage that comes with it. Job says, "Not on my watch."

The Moment of Decision

Deciding what your eyes will see is not a decision you make when you see something. You don't make it when you see the short skirt. You don't make it when you are browsing the internet. You don't make it when you are watching the movie. It's a pre-decision you authenticate when you see something. The decision to look away and not look back, because that's the kind of man you have chosen to be. The decision to have men you trust hold you accountable by giving them the passcodes to your phone because you have determined to be free and stay free. The decision to hard pass on movies with sex scenes and nudity, because you are not the kind of man who pays people to undress on camera so you can watch.[17] Those decisions aren't made in the moment; they flow from a covenant with your eyes that you establish in God's presence.

That's why this can't just be a resolution to do better or try harder. It's something you have to ask God for the strength to do. With King David we have to pray, "Turn my eyes from looking at worthless things; and give me life in your ways."[18]

What Gets Your Attention?

Where we look is always the result of what has our attention, and attention is something we give. We use phrases like "caught my eye," "you have my attention," or "my eyes were glued to the screen." The very language we employ speaks to the reality that we allow certain images to capture us. Perhaps this is why King David asked God to turn his eyes from looking. Couldn't he turn his own eyes away? No, he couldn't, and neither can you. Willpower might work on occasion, but the fact is that some images are just too captivating (in the most literal sense of the word) for you to consistently look away. And like so many things in life, the more you allow "worthless" things in, the easier it becomes for those things to gain unfettered access to your heart.

So, the question is: what gets your attention?

We either devalue our own engagement by giving our attention to what is worthless, or we intentionally choose to upgrade the intake of our eyes to what is befitting of the temple of the Holy Spirit. Your consistent "yes" to the Spirit of God will build the muscle of yielding to the Spirit's voice. Many people struggle to hear God's voice or discern if and when He is speaking because they haven't built the muscle memory of obedience. They have been far better at making excuses and allowances for their flesh than at walking in holiness. One of the best ways to hone that sensitivity to God's voice is by allowing Him to train your eyes because our world is constantly putting images in front of us that necessitate immediate obedience to the Holy Spirit. And an amazing thing will happen as you give God your consistent "yes" and begin to consciously value yourself by getting choosy about what you allow to capture your attention: God will teach you to see through the darkness.

Eyes Like a Lion

For some reading this, your visual diet has consisted of darkness for so long that it's hard for you to imagine looking at the world without that filter. The good news is that God not only wants to empower you to turn your eyes from looking at worthless things but He also wants to help you train yourself to see through the darkness around you. Lions aren't just the kings of the jungle because they are bigger, stronger, and more ferocious than the other species that populate the animal kingdom. Those traits are important, but it's those attributes combined with the capabilities of their eyes that make them particularly deadly. Lions and humans have essentially the same quality of eyesight during the day, but lions see eight times better at night. This is because of a biological trait known as *tapetum lucidum*.[19] This means their eyes have a highly reflective layer behind their retina, so the darkness doesn't stop them or render them helpless. Instead, when darkness descends, they become even more of what they already are. Moonlight hits the white layer under their eyes, causing their pupils to dilate and giving them the night vision they need to hunt.[20] The absence of light does not rob them of any of their king-of-the-jungle capabilities, it just makes all of those traits more intimidating because they can see you even if you can't see them. Not even the blackest night keeps them from their task because they can see through the darkness.

As a follower of Jesus, you already possess this capability, not biologically but spiritually. Your heart has eyes, which admittedly sounds a bit weird, but it's true. That's why the apostle Paul said that you need to have "the eyes of your hearts enlightened."[21] In other words, you need the spiritual night vision that is available in Christ. The opening verses of the Gospel of John allude to this reality in the coming of Jesus: "The light shines in the darkness, and the darkness can never extinguish it."[22] But it gets better, because later in the New Testament we read this shocking statement in the letter to Corinthian Christians: "For God, who said, 'Let light shine out of darkness,' made his light shine in our hearts."[23] The same light that radiated from Christ has not only lit up the darkness of our hearts but works through us to light up the darkness around us.[24] The light you carry in you illuminates the darkness around you. In this sense, you have spiritual *tapetum lucidum* (which sounds awesome). It's the power the Holy Spirit has given you by virtue of His presence in you, so that in a dark world you don't stumble around or live blinded by the darkness that surrounds you. Look at the way the psalmist describes God's perception of the darkness: "Even the darkness is not dark to you; the night is bright as the day, for darkness is as light with you."[25]

Instead of being overwhelmed, confused, and paralyzed by darkness, you can look through the murkiness of circumstances, conversations, and conflict to discern what's actually going on. Our guess is that you probably know someone who seems to have the preternatural ability to see through the confusion and chaos of situations they encounter, and perhaps you have wondered how they do that. Are they just extra wise? Or could it be that they are pressing into the power that as a Christian you already possess? The answer is yes and yes. The wisdom they wield is in large part due to them tapping into the supernatural supply that you also have access to. But this light that Christ has caused to shine in your heart not only allows you to see through the darkness, it also lights up the darkness around you. In other words, people should be able to see better when you are around. Remember, Jesus said you are the light of the world. You are a carrier not only of the metaphorical light of the gospel but also of the light that exposes and expels darkness. Every environment you step into should be illuminated by the light of the gospel emanating from your heart, and consequently those environments should also look different to the people around you because of the light you carry.

Right Side Up in an Upside-Down World

The power God gives us to see through the darkness around us not only lights up the pitch-black that blankets our broken world but it also gives us a perspective on our upside-down culture. If you look around and wonder if society has lost its mind, it has. We live in a world that celebrates darkness, perpetuates confusion, and trumpets moral relativism. The cultural push toward the destruction of our foundations, namely faith and family, is moving at breakneck speed. Which means that if you are a heterosexual male who believes the Bible, loves Jesus, and lives like it, you will be viewed as weird and maybe dangerous.

Your perspective will be sidelined. Your values will be characterized as bigoted and hateful. Your standards and morality will be seen as backward. Because we live in an upside-down world in which Satan is constantly seeking to counterfeit what God has created.

All of this means that we have a choice. We can either choose to wring our hands and air our concerns and frustrations through every available outlet, or we can do the harder thing. We can stand for truth with the lives we live. The psalmist asks this question: "If the foundations are destroyed, what can the righteous do?"[26] He immediately follows this question up with a declaration of God's character and kingship. In other words, we can look around and get worried, uptight, and angry, or we can trust God and live in light of the fact that He is on the throne. Satan loves to stir confusion and chaos, so men of God have to stand as a bulwark against the enemy's agenda. We have to be more vigilant than ever about framing their existence through the lens of biblical convictions and clarity. You may already know this, but one of the mind-blowing truths about the way the human eye works is that it sees everything you look at upside down in 2D, but your brain flips the image right side up and makes it 3D. A lionhearted man is constantly doing the same thing. Our culture is continually dispensing and commending anti-Christ images, narratives, and values that we have to recognize and put into proper perspective.

We have to see differently because we are different. We have to see through the eyes of our heart. We have to look away from evil and see through the darkness. We have to fix our eyes on Jesus. To live lionhearted, we have to see that way.

09

Where Lions Tread

Ponder the path of your feet; then
all your ways will be sure.

Proverbs 4:26 ESV

It's a dangerous business, Frodo, going out your door.
You step onto the road, and if you don't keep your feet,
there's no knowing where you might be swept off to.

J. R. R. Tolkien, The Fellowship of the Ring

Weeks of poor planning had led to this moment. The setting was a dilapidated house that reeked of burnt plastic. Two officers from Detroit's Twelfth Precinct took turns sitting, standing, and pacing while they waited. They were positioned to catch the buyers they had worked to lure to this address under the pretense that they were dealing dope. The plan was to arrest their would-be customers and seize their vehicles. If all went well, the operation would be a big win for this drug-infested neighborhood and the department. So they waited.

Not far from this location, surveillance was underway, but the target wasn't the buyers but the sellers. Officers from Detroit's Eleventh Precinct had been watching a house. Their intel said dealers were using this house as a distribution point. The plan was to approach the house, arrest the dealers, and confiscate the product.[1]

After pulling up in front of the run-down house, they did their best to move toward the door without raising suspicion. Everything was going according to plan. But just then, chaos ensued. Both groups began yelling the exact same thing: "Police! Get on the ground! Do it now!" There was yelling, punching, more yelling, guns drawn, and threats made. As the officers attempted to arrest each other, the homeowner stood nearby and watched this real-life Keystone Cops moment unfold.

Thankfully, the only casualties were egos. The investigation that followed ended with officers suspended and departments embarrassed. Police Chief James Craig's statement said simply, "This is probably one of the most embarrassing things I've seen in this department since I've been appointed police chief. . . . In fact, I'd have to tell you it is probably one of the most disappointing things I've experienced in my entire 40-year career."[2] This would be a hard day to forget. They didn't do the due diligence of pondering the path of their feet. They were caught up in the moment, moving in a direction that was potentially lethal and definitely unwise, and unfortunately they were also unaware.

Call it funny, sad, or mortifying, but don't be too quick to judge. We can all find ourselves in similar places or situations, and though they are not as volatile, they are just as dangerous. How? Simply by getting on the wrong path, by not pondering where we are allowing our feet to take us.

The Path to Happiness

We have already established that the path is not the problem, but the writer of Proverbs is not content with simply telling his son and every one of us to look straight ahead. He is aware that where we are looking is not the only issue that has the potential to derail our hearts and direct our lives. The places we physically go, the people we get close to, and the environments we inhabit make a massive difference in determining what happens at the core of who we are. This is a major theme not just in Proverbs but throughout what is called the wisdom literature of the Old Testament, which includes the Psalms. If you have read the Psalms, then you may be tempted to think that it's just a bunch of poetry, but don't forget that most of what you are reading are the reflections of a battle-hardened warrior king named David. This is a guy who experienced legendary victories and gut-wrenching defeats. People literally wrote and sang songs about him killing tens of thousands of enemy soldiers in battle. Not exactly your stereotypical angst-ridden twentysomething doing a poetry reading on open mic night down at the local coffee shop. Consequently, the Psalms are packed with real-world, life-and-death, combat-tested wisdom, and they begin by speaking to where we go.

These are King David's first words in Psalms: "Blessed is the one who does not walk in step with the wicked or stand in the way that sinners take or sit in the company of mockers."[3] When you read "blessed" in this verse, it's a Hebrew word that means "happy." Happiness is something everyone wants but few people seem to find. Look around: most men are depressed, defeated, frustrated, or angry. But Psalm 1 is the pathway to happiness, and with this statement we can already hear someone saying, "God doesn't care if you are happy. He just wants you to be holy." First, you're wrong. Second, holiness leads to happiness. This idea that kicks off the entire collection of Psalms is kind of staggering.

Tim Keller speaks to why it is so hard for so many of us to believe happiness is something that is supposed to characterize our lives.

> The first thing we see from this text is that blessedness is possible. Happiness is possible. . . . That's a thunderous statement. What do you think of that statement? It's a way of testing where you are. . . . If you say, "Well, of course, happiness is possible," it tells you something about you. Let me tell you what it tells you. Unless you've had an unusually harsh childhood, almost all of us start out thinking happiness is natural in life. "Yes, of course, there are unhappy people, but they've screwed up." Most of us start out thinking happiness is natural. As you grow up you hear all these dire warnings from your parents about how hard things are out there. "You'd better save that money instead of spending it like that," and "Life

is tough." You think, "If I'm good enough, if I'm smart enough, if I'm hard-working enough or whatever. . . . Happiness is natural. . . . That's where we start, and as time goes on, we migrate. After a while, as we begin to see and experience more and more life, we begin to realize happiness isn't anywhere near as easy as we thought. . . . We start out thinking happiness is natural; we end up thinking happiness is unachievable.[4]

As one of our college professors liked to say, "Life is hard and then you die." But this nihilistic view of happiness isn't biblical. That's what the first verse in Psalms is getting at. You can choose the path to happiness. It's not shallow. It's not naive. It's not just whistling in the dark. God made you to experience a happiness that could seem absurd for anyone simply walking through life governed by the chaos of the world around them. The question is: How? What kind of life leads to happiness?

Wrong People, Wrong Path

We both agree that one of our least favorite experiences is missing an exit on a road trip. Like most men, we are in a battle against time (which our wives do not understand or care about). We are in a race to beat Google Maps' estimated time of arrival, and we strongly believe there should be trophies awarded when this is accomplished! But getting on the wrong route ruins the whole thing. Notice King David starts with a warning that if you want to be happy, there is a way you do not want to go. He says this happy person "does not walk in step with the wicked."

Sadly, many men do not heed this warning. Now, you might be able to admit you *do* walk with the wicked, but calling anyone "wicked" feels harsh and judgmental. But could it be that's where our problems start? Are we willing to acknowledge that there are toxic people around us, men who are evil? Labeling people as wicked is an incredibly unpopular idea in our cultural moment, but if we are not able or willing to discern where darkness is present, we will fall prey to it.

Certain relationships should never become friendships. Some acquaintanceships should never become deeper relationships. The people you give access to your life to and choose to walk through life with can detour your life. Your marriage might be in major trouble right now all because you walked down to someone's cubicle and struck up a conversation or went out for a drink. Or maybe you aren't in crisis mode yet, but you are toying with the idea of a different path. A former girlfriend showed up in DMs or a high school crush started messaging you. "We're just catching up" is what you keep telling yourself, not wanting to own the fact that you are already in too deep. You might be a single guy who recently lost your job or is failing in school all because you have linked your life to friends who are on the road to nowhere and they are taking you along for the ride.

The writer of Proverbs says, "Ponder the path of your feet."[5] Meaning, take a moment and actually think about where you are currently going and who you are going with. What path are you currently on? It is possible you are sarcastically thinking, "I am reading right now, so I am not on a path currently." Nice, but you are wrong. You

ARE on a path. The question is: Are you headed where you want to go? Is it intentional? Did you get on it because of God's direction and calling or did you swerve onto it haphazardly? Is it taking you toward a great future or will it burn your life to the ground? Are you on the path because you are seeking approval and acceptance from the wrong people or are you on the path because you are confident in who God created you to be?

Where You Walk Becomes Where You Live

Your trajectory can quickly become your destiny. In Psalm 1, David makes the time-tested observation that where you walk rapidly becomes where you live: "Blessed is the one who does not *walk* in step with the wicked or *stand* in the way that sinners take or *sit* in the company of mockers" (emphasis added).[6] Repeated passing interactions with an unwise person can quickly turn into regularly hanging out, and eventually you are doing life together. Charles Spurgeon wrote,

> When men are living in sin they go from bad to worse. At first, they merely *walk* in the counsel of the careless and *ungodly*, who forget God—the evil is rather practical than habitual—but after that, they become habituated to evil, and they *stand* in the way of open *sinners* who willfully violate God's commandments; and if let alone, they go one step further, and become themselves pestilent teachers and tempters of others, and thus they *sit in the seat of the scornful*. They have taken their degree in vice, and as true Doctors of Damnation they are installed.[7]

He is not overstating the point. When you link your life to men who are foolish, evil, and stupid, you become an expert in all the wrong things. Their viewpoint becomes the way you see life. It happens fast, and the sad truth is that once you have decided to sit, it's hard to get back up and walk away. Why? You have camped out with "mockers." The meaning of the Hebrew word includes the idea of a big-talking, sarcastic rebel who delights in mocking what's right, and when that becomes your world, cynicism is the air you breathe. And it all starts with walking down the path of the wrong people. As Solomon warns his son, "Whoever walks with the wise becomes wise, but the companion of fools will suffer harm."[8] Pay attention to the path you take.

The Road Less Traveled

The best clue to the right path is the men who are on it. If you are worried that you might be on the wrong road, all you have to do is look at the men on your right and on your left. Are they swimming upstream or downstream? Are they content to simply go with the flow of culture or are they men of commitment with clear convictions? Are they easily unsettled or are they deeply rooted in biblical truth?

You may not be a poetry guy, but our guess is that you are at least vaguely familiar with the words of Robert Frost's poem "The Road Not Taken."

> Two roads diverged in a wood, and I—
> I took the one less traveled by,
> And that has made all the difference.[9]

It doesn't seem that anyone was ever able to clearly peg where Frost came down on issues of faith, but the words of this poem struck profound scriptural truth.[10]

Jesus said it this way: "Enter through the narrow gate. For wide is the gate and broad is the road that leads to destruction, and many enter through it. But small is the gate and narrow the road that leads to life, and only a few find it."[11] The path of the lionhearted life is narrow. That's not to say that it's only for an exclusive club; it's just that most men choose to go the easy way. In *The Pilgrim's Progress*, John Bunyan puts it this way: "What God says is best, is best, though all the men in the world are against it."[12] Our flesh loves the path of least resistance.

The Path of Least Resistance

You can graduate college, have a job, volunteer at your church, and still be on the path of least resistance. That's the deceptive thing about the path of least resistance. You are technically doing "good" things, but you aren't building anything of substance or going anywhere. You may even object and say, "I am not on that path," because you have *some* resistance. However, you forget it's not the "path of *no* resistance," it's the "path of *least* resistance." It plays out this way. Your boss finds out you lied about a sick day and wants you to come in for a meeting. So you just bail and find a different job. You overextend your finances by purchasing a new car to impress people you don't even know, and now you are living off credit cards instead of living within your means. Your wife wants to get counseling because she doesn't feel connected to you, and rather than listening and working on the issues, you sweep it under the rug and pretend like everything's fine. Least resistance means "resistance is your enemy." You have concluded that anything that doesn't feel good isn't good. Accountability, healthy conflict, endurance, responsibility, and discipline are all no-gos. They are a bad deal for you. They stress you out and don't give you momentary happiness. They trigger your anxiety. They mess with your personal image. The path of least resistance sucks for those on it because the conflicts they desperately try to avoid seem to weasel their way in and get worse and worse. If you are on this path, the best thing you can do is recognize it. Then, as much as possible, stop blaming everyone else and stay planted where you are. Don't move from church to church when they find out you are not quite the saint you've tried to project. Stay. Don't quit your job because your boss is tired of your excuses. Stay and start taking responsibility. Work hard around people who know your tendency to be lazy. Humble yourself and get counseling. Be around people who challenge and encourage you. Take off the mask, and let people know who you really are. The path of least resistance is a weak, lazy path for guys who only like when people think they are better than they really are, and if that's where you have lived, it's time to change course.

If you keep going down the path of least resistance, you are only lying to yourself. How long can that last? You are telling yourself that it's easier and it's not. You are telling yourself you will have less conflict by not facing situations, and that's not how life works. The more you ignore problems, the bigger they get. It's like feeding a baby gorilla—eventually it turns into a thousand-pound terror. You can move to a different location and find new people, but the old saying rings true: "Wherever you go, there you are." Meaning, eventually you need to look in the mirror and say the common denominator in all the failed relationships, the debts, the lost jobs is you. The antidote to all this is to embrace painful but liberating accountability. Embrace repentance. Choose to stop running and stay planted. Surround yourself with people who know your flaws and help you change. Proverbs 27:6 says, "Wounds from a friend can be trusted." God is a surgeon. He will cut you, but He does it to make you stronger.

The Well-Worn Path to Zion

Just because the pathway to the lionhearted life is narrow doesn't mean it's overgrown. Often, it's the well-worn trails that lead to good things. Our families love the national parks, and it's always nice to get the inside track from someone who can tell you where to find the hidden gems that the crowds pass by. The waterfalls most people miss. The canyon vistas few people see. The best places to spot bears. Usually, it's not that the trail is hard to find, it's just that most people are too busy following the crowd. But once you discover it, you not only want your friends to know about it but you want to go back again and again. The trail may not be wide, but it's well-worn.

This is how life works. Where you walk often creates a path both physically and spiritually. You create paths in your heart. That's why giving thought to your path today is so important: it might become the well-worn path of tomorrow. The psalmist says, "Blessed are those whose strength is in you, in whose heart are the highways to Zion."[13] *Zion* might sound artistic or foreign to us, but to the original reader it was full of concrete meaning. Zion was Jerusalem. The city where, in the Old Testament, God Himself chose to dwell. A sacred place of worship where God was especially present. If it was a physical place, then why does David say that our hearts are highways to Zion? It's because our hearts have pathways. When we go somewhere physically, relationally, or emotionally, we are creating a path that is easier to walk the next time you head that direction. Your heart can house paths to places of death or to the powerful, peace-filled presence of God.

Our grandpa is probably the closest person to a saint that you will find on this planet. He and our grandma had the joy of faithfully pastoring churches in towns and cities across America, though at times they also dealt with the pain and hurt inflicted on them by the people they served. Life and ministry were often anything but easy, but through it all, he loved God deeply. He is a prayer warrior and a worshiper. He is faithfully in God's house. He loves his wife. He tells people about Jesus everywhere he goes, so don't even try to stop him. Even in his eighties, he is still on mission. All of this is true, and he also has severe dementia. It has been sad to watch as this disease has slowly taken his mind, at times making it difficult for him to know where he is or who he is talking to. It's a heartbreaking thing to see anyone experience, but especially someone you love. Not long ago he was in the emergency room because eighty-year-old bodies do not always do what they are supposed to. It was an uncomfortable moment because he didn't grasp everything that was happening and really wanted to go home. We put on worship music in the ER, and instantly the presence of God filled the room. The most powerful part of the whole experience was to watch him worship. He went straight into the presence of his King. The well-worn path to Zion he had created through the years was clear as day to him, even though his mind was hazy. The pathways of his heart that he cultivated through lionhearted living still led him straight to the throne of grace.

That's the life we want for you. One day we will all be in a similar situation that, like it or not, is beyond our control. An overwhelming circumstance that makes everything murky and muddy. In that moment you want to be strong. You want your lion heart to carry you forward even when your body is breaking down. You want stability and peace in the storm. You want wholeness in your brokenness. Make the path now. Block off the paths that lead to dead ends and go off cliffs. Walk paths daily that take you into the presence of God. Make your heart a highway to Zion.

Long Obedience in the Same Direction

Years ago, one of our favorite authors, Eugene Petersen, penned what is now a classic called *A Long Obedience in the Same Direction*. If you don't think about long-term outcomes, you will be easily deceived and disappointed. Short-term wins and instant gratification are not the way to win in life. The best things come through preparation, consistency, and discipline. Does it sound boring? Well, we hate to break it to you, but some of it is. However, the results will be much more gratifying than what you can find on the quick fix route. Results like leaving an eternal legacy, raising not just "good" kids but godly adults, experiencing a satisfying marriage, and making a substantial and lasting impact on the lives of the people around you. All of this is part of the lionhearted life and IS possible for you, but not if you don't get serious.

Now when we say, "Get serious," the point is not to make it harder than it is. You are right to think it's not easy, but it is also not impossible. You just need to get seriously intentional. Take to heart the words of Proverbs 14:8: "The prudent understand where they are going, but fools deceive themselves" (NLT). Fools don't want to think about where their decisions are leading, because they are okay with living deceived. When you don't want to know the long-term outcomes, you are lying to yourself by virtue of your unwillingness to face up to the truth. But that's not the pathway of the lionhearted, who understand where they are going because they have determined where they are going. This has nothing to do with trying to control their fate, but it has everything to do with deciding what convictions will guide their steps into the future. Whether your steps up to this point have been careless or careful, you can commit to walking through life differently in the future, but to live out that determination, you don't just need principles—you need a person. You need to see your life through the lens of the original lionhearted man.

PART 3

THE LIONHEARTED LIFE

10

THE Lionhearted Man

A lion sleeps in the heart of every brave man.

Turkish proverb

Let us fix our eyes on Jesus, the author
and perfecter of our faith.

Hebrews 12:2 BSB

The consensus was that the rusty eyesore needed to go. The Eiffel Tower had worn out its welcome. Constructed in 1889 for the Paris Exposition, the structure was originally intended to stand for only twenty years, so by 1925, many Parisians were ready to see it removed from the city's skyline.[1]

So, it was no surprise when André Poisson received an invitation to a confidential meeting at the Hôtel de Crillon from the French Ministry of Posts and Telegraphs. He was a metal dealer, and the letter sent to him was laced with hints of a major project involving the Eiffel Tower.

During the meeting, a high-ranking government official explained that the city could no longer afford the Eiffel Tower's maintenance and had decided to sell it for scrap. All six of Paris's most prominent scrap metal dealers were present, and the competitive atmosphere among them added to the meeting's urgency and legitimacy.

André was taken on a private tour of the monument, where it was subtly suggested that a bribe could ensure his bid would win. In his desire to get the contract, he paid the equivalent of $1.1 million in order to get the deal done, and he left the meeting triumphant, sensing he had secured a once-in-a-lifetime business opportunity.

Within an hour, his money was speeding away from Paris on a train to Vienna in the hands of Victor Lustig, a con man who had just sold the Eiffel Tower by posing as a government official. Sadly, by the time André realized he'd been taken, it was too late, and he was too humiliated to call the cops. He thought he had all of the information, but he didn't.[2]

This book is a guide to the lionhearted life, but as helpful as the book of Proverbs is and as true as everything we have discovered up to this point is, we are still missing mission-critical information. Solomon possessed astounding wisdom. As we have said, Proverbs is a book from a father to a son filled with profound truths about relationships, money, family, work, and culture. There is almost no area of life it doesn't touch. It was something like a collection of ancient life hacks, even for the most everyday situations. Almost all of the pieces to the lionhearted life are there. Yet, though Solomon might have been able to adjudicate everybody else's impossible dilemmas and dispense wisdom for life, his own life turned into a mess. For starters, the dude had seven hundred wives plus three hundred women on the side (that's not good). He dabbled in pagan religions. His life didn't end up reflecting the godly wisdom that he penned under the inspiration of the Holy Spirit.

It's the nature of humanity, in a way: to see one piece of the puzzle with dazzling clarity and be monumentally clueless about something else. When somebody seems to really grasp one thing about life but be fairly disastrous in another area of life, we may still act surprised, but it's really not all that surprising. "We know in part," Paul said.[3] Well, it is especially problematic when the part you don't know is kind of the center of everything.

Jesus > Solomon

Where do we see Proverbs 4:23—let alone the rest of this smorgasbord of wisdom—actually put on display in a life? Sadly, Solomon's life is not where to look. He had wisdom, but he was far from the embodiment of lionheartedness. The thirty-thousand-foot view on Solomon is that he was a really wise king. Zooming in, however, things get significantly more complicated. The king renowned for his wisdom was also the king whose actual acts as a royal include marrying the pagan daughter of Pharaoh (expressly forbidden) and leading the people of Israel into sexually perverse pagan idolatry. His life is a long sad arc of trusting in his own wisdom more than God's.

But, as it is with all of Scripture, the wisdom in Proverbs wasn't only pointing to wisdom and it certainly wasn't pointing to Solomon. The Bible isn't a book of heroes; it's a book about one hero. Proverbs was pointing us to the ultimate personification of wisdom, the perfect embodiment of manhood, Jesus. "While the Gospels demonstrate that Jesus was wise—indeed, wiser than Solomon . . . Jesus is not simply wise; he is also the very incarnation of God's wisdom," writes Tremper Longman III.[4] Who is the one man who brings all of it together, all of the elements that make up the lionhearted life? Who could bring together divinity and humanity, grace and truth, tenderness and fierceness, authority and vulnerability? If you went to Sunday school as a kid, you probably learned that the right answer to almost any question in class was "JESUS!" and it bears out here. He's the only One who has ever been able to hold it all together, which works out, as He is also the One capable of holding all of us together.

The early church sage Augustine writes, "The Old Testament has no true relish if Christ is not understood in it."[5] We like the word *relish*! What Augustine is saying is simply that if you read the Old Testament without Jesus, you are missing out on what makes it make sense, not only in life but specifically in your life. Unlike Solomon, Jesus is "the apex of God's wisdom."[6] According to Paul, "God has united you with Christ Jesus. For our benefit God made him to be wisdom itself."[7] No wonder, then, that Jesus had to explain to His discouraged and disillusioned disciples that He was the culmination of everything they had heard from the Old Testament. Luke says, "Then Jesus said to them, 'You foolish people! You find it so hard to believe all that the prophets wrote in the Scriptures.' . . . Then Jesus took them through the writings of Moses and all the prophets, explaining from all the Scriptures the things concerning himself."[8] It is all about Him. It was always, *always* really all about Him!

The Look of a Lion

Until you see Jesus, you haven't seen the perfect picture of the lionhearted man. Remember, Jesus is called "the Lion of the tribe of Judah." God is depicted as a lion throughout the Old Testament (see Job 10:16; Isa. 31:4; Jer. 50:44; Hosea 5:14; Amos 3:8). But, at the end of the Bible in Revelation, Jesus is called the lion because He is the personification of God's power and strength. Jesus embodied what it looks like to live with power and strength from the inside out. Solomon was not able to bring together all the fragmentary pieces of wisdom that he learned along the way, but Jesus was. And the same Spirit that empowered Jesus lives inside of us. In Acts, Peter says, "God anointed Jesus of Nazareth with the Holy Spirit and with power."[9] In other words, Jesus's life is not a museum piece; His life is a prototype for the lionhearted life. Jesus longs to show us how to live the way that He lived, walk the way that He walked.

The earliest Christians have understood themselves as apprentices of Jesus—as in, they weren't just reading about the disciples, they understood that they too were supposed to be disciples (think: students), learning to live as Jesus lived. They wanted to act and react to the world around them the way Jesus would. So then, for example, the crucifixion isn't just something we believe that Jesus did for us (though that's important!)—we also are told to take up our cross and follow Him.

The way of Jesus, ultimately, is the way of the heart. It's the way of living from the inside out, rather than the outside in. This isn't just isolated to Jesus's "spiritual" life. It extended to His relationships, His emotions, His mindsets, His priorities, His clarity of purpose. It extended into everything!

We're always inclined to the external imitation of a thing (valuable sometimes, but only to a point), as opposed to going down into the depths of a thing. We often think about the heart last, when the way of Jesus is heart first. Jesus made pointed statements about the heart that not only gave voice to profound spiritual truths but also revealed what He saw as the most critical aspects of the heart. You cannot hope to look like the lionhearted God-man unless you understand Jesus's view of the heart.

This is why we see Jesus reinforcing at every turn that we have to "love the Lord your God with all your heart."[10] This is why He tells us that holy living, deep living, comes out of the abundance of the heart (not out of the abundance of the mind, for the professors out there; not out of the abundance of the body, for the gym rats out there).

But what exactly makes the man that is Jesus? What was inside of Him, what shaped His heart, His interior and exterior life? What shaped His affections? There are, of course, a number of different answers to this question, but we want to highlight a few critical ones—specifically, the practices that enabled Jesus's way of living from the heart.

Sons of God

None of us may ever be accused of having the wisdom of Solomon, but here is a way many men can possibly identify with Solomon—Solomon had all kinds of great ideas, but he still basically sucked at relationships. If you need proof of this, look no further than the fact that theoretically the smartest man who ever lived had seven hundred wives and three hundred concubines. You don't have to have a PhD in psychology to recognize that having a healthy relationship with one person in marriage is hard. We have both been married to our best friends for almost twenty years. Marriage is an incredible gift, but having a great marriage is also a ton of work. Healthy relationships take time and investment. So, the idea of having a healthy relationship with seven hundred wives and three hundred concubines is impossible.

There is no shade here for those of you who are the product of broken relationships—God can redeem anything! But the reason a lot of us struggle on a fundamental level with our most important relationships is precisely because we think all we need to do is tweak our external relationships. So we read books on relationships or communication, or listen to podcasts, or talk to a therapist or a life coach, looking for wisdom on relationships. All of that can be good and healthy to a point, but what Jesus knew that a lot of us still don't is that there is a relationship that starts inside of us that ultimately shapes all of the relationships outside of us.

Everything about who Jesus was and what Jesus did came out of the overflow of His relationship with His Father. He cultivated it. It's why He snuck away from the crowds and even the disciples: to tend to that relationship. Going into the secret place in those early mornings with Him was more important than any other place He would go after that—it would set the agenda for all the other places.

If we don't tend to that relationship first, we will look for the people around us to give us validation they simply cannot grant us. Nobody else is meant to tell us who we are. They don't have the power to define us. It's why even really smart, otherwise successful people often have an unending string of broken relationships—you end up constantly almost strip-mining the people around you, looking to find something they are just not able to give.

Jesus was confident in His relationship with His Father. It was the relationship that mattered most to Him, and it was always His highest priority. It was at His baptism that the Father said, "this is my beloved Son, in whom I am well pleased."[11] Jesus had not yet passed the test of the wilderness, much less the cross, nor had he yet performed all the mighty miracles. But He was the object of His Father's delight, His beloved Son. His Father said who He was, and He believed Him—living every moment of His life from the Father's words over Him. He never forgot who He was, never forgot who His Father said He was. While we are not God's "only begotten," if you are in Christ, you are God's son; live the lionhearted life from that awareness.

Many men struggle to live with purpose and passion because of words their biological father said to them and about them, or never said because they were absent. They can't stop hearing "You're a loser," "You're a mistake," "What's wrong with you?," or "You'll never amount to anything." So they spend their entire lives battling against the destructive words of their dad, rather than living from the life-giving words of their heavenly Father. Until you find your ultimate identity in what God says about you, the life you were meant to live will elude you.

Jesus's own confidence in His identity is revealed in His submission to the Father's will. He said He "can do only what he sees his Father doing."[12] What if it were possible for us to live with that same kind of laser-like focus, that same kind of wide-awakeness to our true identity as God's beloved sons? Jesus did, and He isn't keeping the secret of His way of walking in the world from us—rather, He comes to show us the way, show us His way—so that His way can become our way. But this can only happen when we internalize His words so that they become our words because God's words about us shape our words about ourselves and our reality.

We aren't saying this is a silver bullet that will cause the pain of your past to evaporate, but it does have the power to reframe the way you live. Don't lead with trying to fix that person who hurt you or the relationship that's broken; instead, put your focus on your relationship with your Father, the One who tells you who you really are. If you do that, it's guaranteed to affect how you relate to everyone else—this is what it is to live from the heart!

Empower for the Assignment

It's maddening, but this happens to us all the time. The kids are finally in bed. All of the things that have to be done are mostly done. You are about to fall into bed, but before you do, you put your phone on the charger, only to wake up in the morning and find it wasn't plugged in. Apparently, someone in your family (the guilty shall remain nameless) swiped the little white box that connects to the outlet. It's how too many of us live much of our lives: disconnected from the ultimate source of our power but still busy, still in constant motion, blissfully (or not so blissfully) unaware that we are not plugged in.

This is why it's not enough to get clear on what we are supposed to be doing with our lives—we've got to stay connected to the source that powered the earthly life and ministry of the Son of God. Jesus certainly had clarity of purpose, but part of what set Jesus apart was that He both understood His assignment and depended on a power beyond Himself to fulfill the assignment.

Jesus was empowered for His assignment. He both saw what He was supposed to do and trusted the Spirit of God to give Him the power to actually do it. The anointing of the Holy Spirit that He carried set the tone of His entire life. It's why the first image we get of Jesus's public ministry in Luke 4 is when He reads aloud the words of the ancient prophecy: "The Spirit of the Lord is on me, because he has anointed me to proclaim good news to the poor. He has sent me to proclaim freedom for the prisoners and recovery of sight for the blind, to set the oppressed free, to proclaim the year of the Lord's favor."[13] At that point He rolled up the scroll and sat down—which is the first-century way of dropping the mic. Because Jesus was *that* guy. He was the One anointed by the Spirit to bring good news to the poor, liberate the captives, heal the sick, and uncage the oppressed. He was also the One who breathed the Holy Spirit onto His disciples so that they could live the same way.

The extraordinary thing was that this open secret of the Spirit-filled life wasn't like a pretentious influencer saying, "Hey, look at my awesome house/awesome car/awesome wife/awesome stuff you don't have, sucka." No, the same presence that empowered Jesus, animated Jesus, moved in and through Jesus, is the Spirit that He breathed onto His disciples. He told them it would be even better for them when He went away, because the same power that was in Him would now be in them! The reason that many Christian men are content to live absent of that same power is that Christianity at large has fostered an expectation that a powerless Christianity is the best you can hope for. It no longer bothers us that our lives don't look like the lives of the earliest Christians. We would never dream of seeing a paralyzed person begging for spare change and say, "In the name of Jesus, rise and walk," and if someone did, many Christians would label them a charlatan. Any expectation of walking in the same supernatural power that characterized the life of Christ and His earliest disciples seems to have been drained from the modern church. We have contented ourselves to be carriers of the gospel without any demonstration of its power, and in that way we have become the picture that C. S. Lewis painted in his book *The Weight of Glory*: "We are half-hearted creatures . . . like an ignorant child who wants to go on making mud pies in a slum because he cannot imagine what is meant by the offer of a holiday at the sea. We are far too easily pleased."[14] Jesus's embodiment of the lionhearted existence beckons men to rediscover the only power that can hope to fuel the life they are called to live. Jesus never settled at the level of the expectations of the people around him, and neither can we. He didn't do anything apart from the authority and power of the Holy Spirit, and we don't have to do anything apart from that power either.

What Are You Full Of?

What does it mean to be a man? Since this is a guidebook for men, that's probably a pretty important question. The truth is that everything you have read up to this point is constructing an answer. What can get super tedious is all the stereotypical stuff that people try to tell us about what it means to be masculine. We get a bunch of clichés, like that it's masculine to ignore pain, or that it's not manly to cry, or that it's masculine to be self-sufficient, or not manly to need anybody or anything else. When this becomes our grid, we traffic in a lot of false choices.

It is far better to continue to build out our definition by going back to Jesus, and Scripture describes Him as someone who was "full of grace and truth."[15] He showed grace where the religious wouldn't and spoke truth even when it was costly. We can't overstate how crucial this is. He didn't condemn the woman caught in adultery. He asked that same woman, "Has no one condemned you?" and told her to go and sin no more.[16] His very way of being in the world exposed the hypocrisy of the pious religious leaders around Him. Children ran to Him, but the Roman Empire was terrified of Him. He was popular at parties (His first miracle in John's Gospel was turning water into wine, after all) and unpopular with the religious crowd (they tended to want Him dead). He was compassionate to those life had beaten down, and relentless in His commitment to speak truth. He was not either/or, He was both/and. He showed us that in the lionhearted life, grace and truth aren't mutually exclusive; rather, one informs the other. There is no grace without truth, and there is no truth without grace. No wonder they didn't ever seem to know how to peg Him, and they won't know how to peg you if you follow this way either!

See, the trouble with a lot of pop culture manliness is that, like so many other things in life, it's driven by appearance. If I can buy custom boots like Raylan Givens wears on *Justified* or like Clint Eastwood in *The Good, The Bad and The Ugly*, am I now a lawman or an outlaw? You can buy a cologne that smells like leather and bourbon, but it does not infuse you with manliness. You can be a CrossFit champion and still lack the strength and courage to fulfill the calling on your life. This is why the example we get from Jesus as a man is so different from any of the alternatives—Jesus wasn't trying so hard. He wasn't striving. He wasn't after an image; He was living from the inside.

This is why it's dumb to try to reduce being a man to random stereotypes of manliness. Jesus wept when His best friend died, but He didn't open His mouth when He was on the precipice of death—because there is a time to cry, and there is a time to be silent and do what you came to do. This is the thoroughly wild thing about Jesus being described as both the Lamb of God and the Lion of the tribe of Judah. It wasn't weird for Him to transition between flipping over tables and cleaning out the temple with a whip and taking time to hold little children and speak blessing over their lives. Being a man isn't a simple "always be this way, never be that way"—it's knowing how to be exactly who and what the situation at hand requires to evidence the heart of God.

What if it were possible to be the sort of person who would bear the weight of the cross that you are called to carry for the sake of our mission, without complaining or bad-mouthing anybody, and yet also be the kind of person who is unashamed to weep when your friend dies? What if it were possible to brave the wilderness for forty days and forty nights while staring down the devil and be the kind of person who is filled with compassion when you see the needs of people? What if you didn't have to choose between being vulnerable and being powerful? What if you didn't have to choose between grace and truth? You don't, but you do have to go to school on Jesus's way of seeing people and living the truth. You do have to learn to live from the inside out.

Service and Sacrifice

We aren't trying to get all Yoda on you here, but there's something else you need to know about this way of the heart, and it may in fact sound a little like some Jedi master wisdom: you can't have the life you want by trying to get the life you want. It's indirect. As Jesus put it, you have to lose your life to find it.

More than anything else, this is the heart of Jesus: laying down His own life for us. The way He lived was the way He died. The way He died was the way He lived. The cross was not a detour or cosmic oversight but a pure extension of how He always, always lived. Ultimately, THE lionhearted man came to serve and sacrifice. Serving reveals so much about the current position of your heart and determines so much about the future state of your heart. Serving has a profound way of exposing things that have lingered under the surface.

You can't look like Jesus without sacrifice. It is an essential element of the lionhearted life. Our world has progressively drifted toward a view of sacrifice that implicitly asks, "What's in it for me?" We are less and less inclined to embrace sacrifice when the person's benefit is unclear. But the way of Jesus was never aimed toward personal gain; it was always moving in the direction of the cross.

This is the idea that separates this book from all the health and fitness gurus, life coaches, podcasters, and all-around influencers and content-generators who say a lot of (sometimes helpful and sometimes unhelpful) things about masculinity—the focus of this book isn't ultimately on you. It's ultimately about the impact that your lionhearted living will have on the lives of the people around you. We happen to think that giving yourself away is the way to be the absolute best version of you. That doesn't mean you need to go around looking to make arbitrary sacrifices, trying to prove to yourself or to anybody else how tough you are or how much you can do without (in fact, we decisively don't recommend this). God desires "mercy, not sacrifice" anyway, so there are no merit badges for giving up random things you like to do.[17] Far from being dreary and depressing, this is actually the secret of the "abundant life" Jesus said He came to give us: we are learning how to be image bearers of the living God by learning not to focus on ourselves but to make our entire aim living to please God and to serve people.

Eat Like Jesus

"That sounds awesome . . . but I am not Jesus!" YES, WE KNOW YOU ARE NOT JESUS. We are also not Jesus, and the people closest to us are very confident about this (and they remind us when necessary). Sure, Jesus is unique as the sinless, only begotten Son of God. But the way of Jesus, the path of Jesus, is not unique at all—it's intended to be the way that we live, the path that we walk.

Keep in mind, the way of Christlikeness is not like, say, being an Elvis impersonator. It's not about putting on the right clothes, getting the accent just right, the moves just right. We aren't called to do an impression of Jesus; we are called to live from the heart the way that He did—to live from His heart, the heart that now animates us. The very earthy language of the church in the New Testament gets far too often relegated to hazy, abstract metaphors—we are now THE BODY of Christ. Note the physicality of that: He breathes through us, speaks through us, touches through us. His affections are becoming our affections, His desires are becoming our desires, and His words are becoming our words.

But again, since who He is and who we are can feel like a long way off—how is any of this possible? How do we actually get there, to this new way of living and being in the world? Being like Jesus doesn't simply come down to aspirational thoughts and lofty goals. In many ways, it comes down to feasting on the same things that fed Him, being sustained by the things that sustained Him. Jesus said, "I have food to eat that you know nothing about."[18] What is that food?

Keep in mind that what God wants is people who are humble and hungry. It is not the righteous who will be filled but those who hunger and thirst for righteousness. As we get ready to explore the "diet" of Jesus next, it seems especially right that so much of this life with God comes down to what we hunger for and who we hunger for. It doesn't mean you don't ever crave junk food. It doesn't mean you have reached the place were God is all you want all the time. Sometimes it may not even be *want* so much as *wanting to want*. God did not put this desire for something more—for a life that is more savory, more full, more satisfying—only to leave you to starve in the wilderness. God would not give you these desires if He didn't intend to satiate them. Not only does Revelation give us a glimpse of a future feast but there is a table that is spread before you, here and now in the wilderness, with the bread of life and a cup of salvation. "You prepare a table before me in the presence of my enemies."[19] You are still in the fight, but there is food for the fight—there is bread in the wilderness!

We want to invite you to join us in this prayer:

God, I hear You calling me to the feast. The things I have fed myself do not sustain me. I hunger for the life hidden in Christ—the life that You have prepared for me. I want to feed on You, feast on Your words, drink of Your living water. Where I do not yet long, I long for the longing. What I do not yet want, I want to want. I am tired of things that do not satisfy. Create in me the hunger that only You can fill. Amen.

Now, it's time to look at the diet of the lionhearted life!

11

The Carnivore Diet

You are what you eat.

French proverb

My son, be attentive to my words;
incline your ear to my sayings.

Proverbs 4:20 ESV

You know you are seriously hangry when law enforcement
gets involved. Both of us worked in restaurants. Both of
us have dealt with customers who were less than happy.
Both of us have been left with bad tips or no tip at all.
But we are proud to say that neither of us has ever had
the cops called on us for bad service, which is less than
the employees at a Waco McDonald's can say.

The future 911 caller came through the drive-thru line simply as a woman with her heart set on chicken nuggets. She placed her order and waited. Admittedly, fast food is supposed to be fast, and when the speed with which her food was delivered did not meet her standards, she didn't yell at the employees while fishtailing out of the parking lot. She put her car in park in the middle of the line, blocking the customers behind her, and called the police. We aren't sure how the dispatcher relayed this "emergency" to the officers who responded. ("Um, we have a delay on a ten-count nugget in progress.") According to the hangry customer, the crime in question was that the nuggets had taken too long. With the cars behind her being held hostage, she was demanding that the tardy nuggets be free. In response to the situation, Sgt. W. Patrick Swanton from the Waco Police Department said, "We definitely have better things to do than respond to a call about chicken nuggets not being served quickly enough."[1] The lady ended up exiting the drive-thru line with a refund but without the nuggets that she had waited so long to enjoy.

The Diet of Desire

Your body wants what it wants because you have trained it to want certain things. What you eat is a matter of habit. Day to day, we aren't making massive changes to the kind or quality of food we are feeding on. Even if you are eating fast food, you are probably gravitating back to the same two or three drive-thru lines again and again. Why? You are eating out of habit. For many of us, the routine that dictates our diets was created subconsciously. Our cravings have been reinforced by the neurotransmitter dopamine.

It's the built-in reward system of our bodies that motivates repeated behavior; that is, the creation of a habit. The food industry has worked to use this biological reality to their advantage by cultivating an appetite for the ideal mixture of fat, sugar, and salt.[2] This neurological response rewarding our junk food intake even plays off our happy memories, linking them to food we just can't stop eating.[3] All of this is reinforcing our dietary preferences under the radar of our conscious realization. Now, we need to pause and acknowledge that we are not nutritionists, and this is not a book about food, but the way most of us eat serves as a perfect metaphor for the way appetite functions in every other area of our lives, including spirituality.

Most of us would likely admit that a steady intake of sugar, fat, and salt is not helping us become the ideal versions of ourselves. But we just keep eating. We do it out of desire. We want what we want, and those cravings are usually fueled by the wrong things. Stress, business, and fatigue end up driving our decisions, and those decisions dictate our desires. If we are not careful, our lives become an infinite loop of responding to negative pressures with actions that feel good in the moment but build bad habits for our future. It's not that desire is wrong. It's a God-given tool. It's the hunger pain of life. The issue is: Are you intentionally fostering your desire for the best in life, or have you cultivated an appetite for something less?

A Lionhearted Appetite Leads to Lionhearted Habits

Jesus was motivated by appetite. He said, "My food is to do the will of him who sent me and to accomplish his

191

work."[4] He wasn't a robot. He was moved by hunger. It's woven into the fabric of what it means to be human, and this is why Jesus appeals to people on this basis. Look at Jesus's words in John 6:35: "I am the bread of life. Whoever comes to me will never go hungry, and whoever believes in me will never be thirsty." This is also why the Bible calls us to "taste and see that the LORD is good."[5] God knows that we are moved by appetite, so He invites us to pursue Him on the basis of satisfying our hunger. However, just because something is good or even the best doesn't necessarily mean we will crave it.

The best things in life are an acquired taste. As dads, both of us know this simply by watching our kids. Nobody had to teach them to like candy. We never had to force them to eat their ice cream. But we had to teach them to appreciate a pan-seared, oven-finished, perfectly cooked filet mignon. Otherwise, they would have picked a Reese's Peanut Butter Cup instead. The same is true with us. You have to acquire and cultivate a taste for what is best. Then, as you consciously choose to satisfy yourself with fare made from the highest quality ingredients, you find that this becomes not only what you know you need but also what you want. Jesus's appetite led to a lifestyle, and when you eat off the same spiritual menu that nourished the Son of God, you create the lionhearted habits that sustain the lionhearted life.

Not by Bread Alone

Lions need meat, lots of it. Male lions consume up to 15 pounds of meat a day. But if they have gone without food for a while, they can also eat up to 110 pounds of meat in one sitting.[6] The fact is you need meat, too, and lots of it. One of the first recorded statements from Jesus in the Gospels is about food: "man shall not live on bread alone."[7] Admittedly, ripped out of context it could sound like a plug for Keto. But this quote from the Old Testament that He threw back at Satan in response to His first wilderness temptation had nothing to do with reducing your gluten intake. When He said, "Man shall not live on bread alone, but on every word that comes from the mouth of God,"[8] He was obviously pointing to a spiritual principle. You can't really live unless what sustains your life consists of more than physical nourishment. Be as healthy as you want. Count your calories. Cut out sugar. Eat clean. But if that's all you are feeding on, you will basically be "mostly dead," to borrow a phrase from *The Princess Bride*. At the moment Jesus makes this retort to the devil, our guess is that He is hungrier than you have ever been. He's at the tail end of a forty-day fast, but in describing Jesus's condition, Matthew uses a comical economy of words. He simply says, "He was hungry."[9] If you are like us, that statement makes you smile. You are probably thinking, "I'll bet He was!" And yet, our hunch is that Matthew may be driving home a point. Jesus wasn't eating, but He wasn't starving. Something was nourishing Him, and that something was the words of God.

New Testament scholar John Nolland nails it when he says, "Listening to God . . . is life-sustaining."[10] Embedded in this truth is the reality that none of our lives are merely physical. As our dad so often says, "The spiritual realities are the greater realities." Anyone who has developed a deep walk with God knows this because they have lived it. Scientists tell us that carbon, hydrogen, nitrogen, oxygen, phosphorus, and sulfur are "the building blocks of life."[11] Yet, Jesus knew that the lionhearted life, the life that every man has been created to live, is unsustainable without the words of God.

You feast on that not only through reading, meditating on, and memorizing Scripture but also by keeping your heart in tune with the Holy Spirit. In concert with and under the authority of His Word (the Bible), God also wants to speak to you personally through the circumstances of your life. Hearing His voice is not a luxury. It's a necessity. You need to be looking for Him to speak to your heart every day, and as pastor Chris Hodges says, "If I don't get a word from God at least every four to five days, then I know something is wrong."[12] It could be a verse from your Bible reading that jumps off the page. It could be a sense that God is directing you regarding something you have prayed about. It could be something God says to you through another person. God loves to talk to people, and you need to anticipate that God wants to speak to you and position yourself to listen. This starts with being in the Bible every day. Otherwise, you will end up living a malnourished Christianity that is devoid of the strength that characterized THE lionhearted God-man, Jesus Christ. He is the prototype for every man following His footsteps into a lionhearted existence, and if He needed the Word of God, you need the Word of God.

Not Just Knowing, It's Doing

It doesn't matter how healthy your diet is, if you are loading up your plate then planting yourself on the couch all day, there are going to be problems. You need to move. Nutrition provides energy that needs to manifest itself in activity. If this sounds like common sense almost to the point of being embarrassingly simple, it is. However, the truth is that too many men are feasting on God's Word but putting very little of it into action. Jesus made another dietary statement in the Gospels, which is essential to the lionhearted life. He told his disciples, "My food is to do the will of him who sent me and to accomplish his work."[13] The early church father Augustine translated Jesus's words, "My meat, to do the will of Him that sent Me."[14] Jesus knew that putting truth into practice is the way we metabolize God's Word. Jesus also understood that consuming large amounts of biblical truth and doing nothing with it is dangerous.

The path to pride, hypocrisy, and self-righteousness is knowing a lot and doing little. To know and not live is a deadly combination. This is the recipe for a Pharisee. If that's a new word for you, those were the guys who followed Jesus around criticizing His message and ministry. Douglas Wilson helpfully articulates the four main traits of the Pharisees we meet in the New Testament (and today): (1) a feeling of superiority, (2) a superficial understanding of the necessity of forgiveness, (3) an exaggerated view of fairness, and (4) an unteachable spirit.[15] They were varsity-level spiritual armchair quarterbacks. Today, these are the men (we are using that term loosely) who feel their contribution to the world is critiquing other Christians. They love throwing their theological weight around. They build their platforms and personas on picking people apart in the name of exposing error. They are kings of clickbait and petty jabs, but the problem is that their chosen calling is primarily reflected in the group of people who most violently opposed Jesus. The Son of God didn't weaponize the truth to attack His enemies; He lived it and preached it for the sake of a lost and dying world. When you are more in love with how the truth can serve your agenda than how through serving you can embody the truth, something is wrong.

We love the Bible and feast on theology. But if a major part of our daily diet doesn't consist of putting God's Word into practice in ways that demonstrate Jesus's sacrificial love for the church and heart for the lost, our diet is deficient. Too often Christians have fashioned God's Word into a battle-ax for the sake of scoring points and winning arguments rather than wielding it as the sword of the Spirit for the purpose of doing damage to darkness. Scripture should constantly be producing humility, moving us to serve people, and fueling our love for God. If those things aren't happening, then our application of biblical truth no longer looks like the way of Jesus. The lionhearted life typified by the Son of God was truth in action.

Time in Lonely Places

What allows the Word of God and your work for God to continually nourish your life? As surprising as this may sound, those two things are woefully insufficient to feed the life of ferocious faith you were created to live. That's why Jesus so consistently pulled away to spend time in prayer.

If you want to be like Jesus, you have to take your cues for life from the way He lived, and the people who watched Jesus closely knew He often withdrew. He went away to pray. Luke made this observation about Jesus's routine: "Jesus often withdrew to lonely places and prayed."[16] He was modeling a powerful truth. All of us need time in lonely places. Every day you have to make space to be with God. As John Flavel writes, "Cultivate a habit of communion with God. This will prepare you for whatever may happen."[17] He's not wrong. You have no idea what a given day will hold or what wisdom you will need to apply God's Word to a situation you will face. The only way you can hope to be ready for the unknown, let alone the unrelenting attack of the enemy, is by spending lonely time in God's presence. Writing to young men, J. C. Ryle says, "If you are to resist the world, the flesh, and the devil, you must pray."[18]

Getting alone with God is essential. The idea here is not just getting away from other people—some of us would prefer that anyway (God bless all the introverts reading this book!). The Greek word translated "lonely" is *erémos*, which can also find its English equivalent in the words *forsaken*, *abandoned*, and *deserted*.[19] Prayer at its best requires abandoning the things that get in the way of prayer. Your phone is probably a good place to start. But often, the barriers to deep communion with God are not just physical but mental and emotional.

We continually allow our stress, anxiety, and worries to monopolize our conversation with God. On the one hand, that is the best place to bring those burdens, but the problem is that usually instead of casting those cares on God, we allow them to dominate our time with Him. When that happens, it sucks the life out of what should be the most life-giving part of your day. This would be the result in any relationship where all you ever did was dump your needs and wants on them and walk away. It's not wrong to tell God what you need, but if that is all you can do, your prayer time has become all about you. Your time with God is at its best when it is about God and praying for the needs of others. But for that to happen we have to consciously abandon our anxiety by saying, "God, I am leaving ____ so I can focus on You." The list of what needs to be deserted as we enter God's presence is as personal as each person praying. You know yourself. You know what distracts you. You are the one who knows what you need to do to focus on your heavenly Father. Maybe it's best to work backward by starting with what is essential. For us, it's the Bible, a journal, a pen, a quiet spot, and coffee (yes, that item is very important). Everything else is negotiable. If you haven't been intentional about withdrawing to lonely places for undistracted time with God, it's time to make this part of your daily diet.

Mentors Wanted Dead and Alive

The menu we have described up to this point is good, but it's missing something. People. Jesus was a people person. You need people in your life. In particular, you need other lionhearted men who are passionately pursuing Jesus around you, or it will be impossible for you to live a lionhearted life. You have probably heard it before, but we are going to say it real loud for the dudes in the back— Christianity is not a do-it-yourself project. A lone-wolf

Christian is a contradiction in terms, plus it doesn't work. Isolated, just-me-and-Jesus type men get weird in a hurry. And if you are thinking, "Am I one of those guys?" you might be but you don't have to be.

Proverbs is full of wise words about the power of community and connection. Solomon is writing to his son because he knew the massive hole that would be in his son's life without other godly men in the mix. That's why he says, "As iron sharpens iron, so one person sharpens another" and "A brother is born for a time of adversity."[20] You need men who have your back and who will get in your face. You need men who love you enough to tell the truth and care about you enough to encourage you when life is hard. You need men in your life who are serious about living the lionhearted life. If you are the most committed follower of Christ in your core group, that's not good. Yes, there should be men you are discipling, but you also need men who are pushing you. This doesn't mean you have to meet up every other day to bare your soul, but it does mean they know enough about your life to tell you when they see something is off.

You need mentors, but not all of them have to be alive. Some of the most impactful voices in our lives are dead guys. As John Piper says, "My main mentors are all dead. There are a few living ones."[21] Find people to read and listen to who pour gas on the fire of what God is already doing in your heart. We have greatly benefited from the works of Tim Keller (died in 2023), John Owen (died in 1683), Smith Wigglesworth (died in 1947), Jonathan Edwards (died in 1758), J. I. Packer (died in 2020), John G. Lake (died in 1935), and the list goes on. All these men are in heaven, but their words are still moving us toward

Christlikeness. There are paragraphs they have written and talks they have given that have profoundly shaped our lives.

Who are the voices, dead and alive, in your life who are calling you deeper? Who is stirring holy dissatisfaction in your heart for staying where you are? Who is keeping you from getting comfortable in your current level of commitment? The lionhearted life requires voices that sharpen you, stretch you, and strengthen you. Find the people who continually compel you to run harder after God and lean into their influence in your life.

Let's Eat

"One cannot think well, love well, sleep well, if one has not dined well."[22] To these famous words from Virginia Woolf, we say, "Amen." This statement is even truer when it comes to your spiritual dining. Your spiritual life will always be a glaring reflection of what you choose to eat. You become what you consume. The building blocks of a lionhearted life are not a mystery. Every man reading this book can live a life that looks like THE original lionhearted man. Writing a letter to some of the first Christians, the apostle Peter said, "[God's] divine power has given us everything we need for a godly life through our knowledge of him who called us by his own glory and goodness."[23] You have what you need. The table is set. It comes down to determining what your diet will be.

12

Ready to Roar

The wicked flee though no one pursues, but
the righteous are as bold as a lion.

Proverbs 28:1

The fear I felt was no rational fear, but a
panic terror not only of the Martians but of
the dusk and stillness all about me. Such an
extraordinary effect in unmanning me it had
that I ran weeping silently as a child might do.
Once I had turned, I did not dare look back.

H. G. Wells, The War of the Worlds

Shotguns were loaded. Men guarded their property, keeping eyes open for invaders. There were reports of mass
stampedes as people fled for safety. Families hurriedly

packed their cars, rushing to escape with their most valuable possessions. Others barricaded themselves in their homes, hoping that they would be spared. It was said that men and women hurried to churches fearing that the end had come. There were even stories of people so terrified that they committed suicide to avoid the global attack. People reported seeing Martians in the streets and hearing the sounds of extraterrestrial beings.

The panic was real, but the reason for the pandemonium was not.

The night before, on October 30, 1938, *Mercury Theatre on the Air* had featured a radio broadcast of H. G. Wells's *The War of the Worlds*. Orson Welles had adapted the story into a series of realistic news bulletins that preempted regularly scheduled programming. The next morning, Welles was front-page news from coast to coast. His radio theater had gone 1930s viral.[1]

People had let their media-induced anxiety get the best of them, believing that an actual alien invasion was in progress as the program aired. The panic quickly subsided, but the story became a cautionary tale of real-life chaos and the consequences that manufactured fears can create.

Phantom Fears

Many of us are fleeing from an idea, not an actual threat. It's the impulse to run from shadows. When we do this, we are only reflecting the reactionary tendency of the world around us. It is a propensity made manifest in our decision-making. You see, fleeing from phantom fears can become a way of life, putting you on a trajectory of timidity.

Fear can exaggerate. Fear can make you see what isn't there. Fear can push you where you would never want to go. But for many men, fear moves them to silence. Yet, because fear is not exactly the manliest thing to admit, it is often left to linger under the surface, unaddressed and unexpressed.

Your lionheartedness is never unleashed because you choose to play it safe rather than roar. A roar is loud and aggressive. Your roar could come across as offensive. Your roar might make people uncomfortable. Your roar could cause people to say, "Who does he think he is?" Your roar could put you on the menu of the cancel culture mob. Your roar could put a target on your back. Your roar might make life harder. So, on the basis of "could" and "might," we are chased into silence and passivity. We are voluntarily caged and muzzled by phantom fears.

This is not to say that those fears can't become reality. They certainly can. It's not that they aren't valid. It's that they don't have the power we perceive them to possess. They are schoolyard bullies who wouldn't ever dream of sticking around to finish the fight. They are a five-pound dog with a fifty-pound bark. But their campaign of intimidation is highly successful. We learn at a young age that to take a stand and make your voice heard is dangerous, and that's a message we internalize. Not only do we hear this narrative around us, but the message begins to echo inside of us. We tell ourselves that someone else will speak up. Someone else will take a stand. Someone else will step up. We strengthen the argument for silence by continually reminding ourselves that this "someone else" will do it better than we can anyway.

Of course, the problem with allowing phantom fears to dictate your decisions is you end up being ruled by an imaginary force that stops you before you even start, and it not only quenches your appetite for public boldness but it erodes your private passion. This erosion quickly seeps into our relationships. Marriage becomes a contract you keep intact for the kids. Parenting becomes an exhausting slog. Your job becomes what you do to pay the bills, counting down the days until you can quit. If what you do doesn't matter and "someone else" is always better suited for the task, then why even try? Perhaps that sounds extreme, but choosing the path of least resistance can easily become a way of life. As the theologian Michael Reeves put it, "Failure and mediocrity can be comfortable and undemanding friends."[2]

That doesn't mean we don't love to talk about taking a stand; it's just harder than it sounds. We want to. We are inspired by the idea. We might even daydream about it. But then we are sucked back into the real world and brought down to reality. As Henry David Thoreau famously writes, "The mass of men leads lives of quiet desperation. What is called resignation is confirmed desperation."[3] We resign ourselves to lives that matter less than we know, deep down, they are meant to. Just work the job, dream about retirement, hope your marriage survives, and maybe, if you're lucky, buy a boat.

But that's not the life you were made for.

Fear of the Right Thing

When we say you were made for more, this isn't some pop psychology motivational mumbo jumbo (we just had to find a place to put "mumbo jumbo" in this book). The goal isn't to give you a pep talk as we get close to the end of this journey together. We want to take you back to the why behind the lionhearted life.

It matters if you roar. Not because God needs another lionhearted man so His kingdom doesn't fall apart. God is perfectly capable of moving redemptive history forward without any one of us; however, He desires to work through us. He didn't create you to coast. He didn't create you to sit on the bleachers of life, eating popcorn, admiring what He is doing through other people. But if what muzzles your roar or pushes you into passivity is the fear of people, your life will be marked by what could have been. Your decisions and your destiny will be dominated by the empty applause of people or the hollow hate of the mob. But our point is not that fear is the enemy. Fear of the wrong thing is the enemy.

Ironically, fear is an essential ingredient to being bold as a lion. Near the center of Proverbs, Solomon pointed his son to the ground zero of the lionhearted life: "The fear of the LORD is the beginning of wisdom, and knowledge of the Holy One is understanding."[4] In fact, the foundation that the Bible's primary book on wisdom builds on is Proverbs 1:7: "The fear of the LORD is the beginning of knowledge, but fools despise wisdom and instruction." But what does the Bible mean when it talks about the fear of the Lord or the fear of God? Is all fear created equal?

The simple answer is no, and this truth is even seen in Solomon's contrast in Proverbs 28:1: "The wicked flee though no one pursues, but the righteous are as bold as a lion." The wicked flee for a lot of reasons, but at the root, they have a sinful fear of God. This sinful fear of God is the sort of fear James tells us the demons have when they believe and shudder.[5] It is the fear Moses wanted to remove from the Israelites at Sinai. It is the fear Adam had when he first sinned and hid from God.[6] Michael Reeves says, "Adam was the first one to feel this fear, and his reaction in that moment shows us its essential nature: sinful fear drives you *away* from God. This is the fear of the unbeliever who hates God, who remains a rebel at heart, who fears being exposed as a sinner and so runs from God."[7] This is the world's fear—the kind of fear that makes it impossible to live lionhearted. It is built on a misrepresentation of who God is and what God is like. A godly fear of the Lord has the opposite effect: it draws us close to God. This is exactly what God said through the Old Testament prophet Jeremiah would happen: "I will make with them an everlasting covenant, that I will not turn away from doing good to them. And I will put the fear of me in their hearts, that they may not turn from me."[8]

The Fear That Equals a Fearless Life

The righteous fear of the Lord not only sees God as He is but fortifies a fearless life. How does it do that? Simply put, it destroys other fears. This was God's message to His people through Isaiah: "Do not call conspiracy all that this people calls conspiracy, and do not fear what they fear, nor be in dread. But the LORD of hosts, him you shall honor as holy. Let him be your fear, and let him be your dread."[9] In other words, when you really fear God, you won't fear what everyone else is afraid of. Even the "conspiracy" terminology Isaiah uses is strikingly applicable to our present cultural moment and the kind of fear and unsettledness that social media is uniquely suited to create. People have allowed their phones to dictate their fears. Every day, new conspiracies built on half-truths, misinformation, and hidden agendas are churned out to stoke confusion, frustration, and rage. Sadly, this has been shown to be very easy to do. The reason this has proven so effective is that the sound bites, viral videos, and clickbait headlines prey on the one fear that opens the floodgate to every other fear—the fear of people.

Fear of the wrong things will always rob you of courage, but fear of God puts steel in your spine. John Bunyan, a Puritan pastor and author who wrote one of the bestselling books of all time, *The Pilgrim's Progress*, introduced his readers to Mr. Godly-Fear, a man of "courage, conduct and valour."[10] Not only is the name "Mr. Godly-Fear" just plain awesome, but this guy has a lot in common with the lionhearted man. These are men of courage and conviction. These are men who are not pushed around by cultural conspiracies or the world's agenda. That kind of stability is one of the greatest gifts a lionhearted man can give to the people around him, starting with his family. Living and leading from the foundation of a fear of God makes you unshakable. It enables you to be the leader that God created and called you to be. This kind of man lives the truth and speaks the truth even when living by principles comes with a price tag. This is a quality our world desperately needs. Men whose lives are built on the solid rock are in short supply, so when you stand your ground by rooting yourself in the countercultural fear of

God, people can't help but take notice of the lion in you. However, for some of us that last sentence would be more applicable in the past tense because that fearlessness is no longer true of us.

Time to Get Your Roar Back

Think about your life. Was there a time when you were more ready to roar? When all our talk about fearlessness felt like a way you could actually live, not a fantasy land? Was there a time when you were less inclined to play it safe? Could it be that a trial you have walked through, trauma you have endured, or tragedy that struck took the wind out of your sails? Life can literally kick the roar out of you. A friend betrays, a relationship sours, a business partner cheats you, a loss blindsides you—any one of those experiences can be incredibly disorienting. The disappointment and pain can put you in a defensive posture. The mantra you begin living by becomes, "I am not going to let that happen again." The problem is that you stop putting yourself out there. Walls go up in relationships and, before long, those walls extend to your walk with God. The appetite for stepping out into the unknown diminishes. You start daydreaming about an easier life. Faith feels too risky. The things you once envisioned doing for God and God doing through you start to seem uncertain and unsafe. Maybe it's just not worth it. Slowly, the lionhearted life begins to sound like a good idea for someone else, just not for you. If that's where you are, then you need to hear two things: (1) you are not alone, and (2) you can't live there.

Jesus is the ultimate lionhearted man, and He is also "a man of sorrows and acquainted with grief."[11] His earthly ministry was filled with relentless haters, people trying to trap Him, and those closest to Him not believing Him. He understands betrayal and backstabbing at the personal level. He gets it. He knows the impulse to recoil. He knows what it's like to see the will of God for your life and ask for an exit ramp. He knows the desire to take an easier way. But He didn't.

Jesus understood something about the kingdom of God that every man of God has to remember: it's not meant to be easy. Silence, passivity, and apathy will always be the world's preference for God's people, especially men. If you are hoping for anything less than a battle when you live lionhearted for the name and the fame of Jesus, it's only because you haven't read your Bible very closely. There is going to be pushback. Spiritual warfare is part of the package, because there is another lion, a counterfeit king, seeking to take territory for darkness. Near the end of the New Testament, Peter said, "Stay alert! Watch out for your great enemy, the devil. He prowls around like a roaring lion, looking for someone to devour."[12] Notice the devil is *like* a lion, but he is a poor imitation of the real thing, the Lion of the tribe of Judah. As author Warren Wiersbe writes, "He is a great pretender. . . . His strategy is to counterfeit whatever God does."[13] Still, the demonic pushback to your roar is real. This is why Jesus's words in Matthew 11 are so apt for every man who has been sidelined into silence: "From the days of John the Baptist until now the kingdom of heaven has suffered violence, and the violent take it by force."[14] In other words, the kingdom belongs to those who fight for it.[15] There is a God-given mandate on the life of every man to advance God's rule and reign and to do damage to darkness. But, to do that, you have to get your roar back.

Confidence in God

Once again, this is not the locker-room pep talk part of this book. We aren't coaches trying to inspire you with clichés to go back onto the field to win the game of life. If this book ended with pages of persuasive paragraphs bent on convincing you of your ability to live the lionhearted life, that would be sad. It would be sad for us because we would have misled you. And it would be sad for you because your confidence would be misplaced. That's not to say that the way you see yourself doesn't matter, it's just that how you see yourself in light of how you see God is so much more important. A. W. Tozer says, "What comes into our minds when we think about God is the most important thing about us . . . and the most portentous fact about any man is not what he at a given time may say or do, but what he in his deep heart conceives God to be like."[16] Biblical history demonstrates this over and over again. It's the people who had great confidence in God, based on their conviction about His character and His nature, who ultimately did great things for God. They didn't necessarily look lionhearted from the outside, and often their lives were littered with issues that would have seemed to disqualify them. But what they all had in common was their confidence in God.

So, maybe we should ask you a question: What comes into your mind when *you* think about God? This deserves taking a moment to put down the book. Perhaps you even need to write out the thoughts that pop into your head. If you are thinking, "I am going to skip this," we know how you feel. We would usually do the exact same thing, but this little exercise has life-changing potential. Just give it five minutes, and don't just write down obvious churchy answers. Put down on paper what is rolling through your mind.

Our guess is that you have never done that before. Now, for another question: Does what you wrote out reflect what the Bible says about who God is? Or maybe an even better question is: Does your life reflect those thoughts?

Ultimately, the righteous aren't bold as a lion simply because of who they are but because they know who their God is. Does a righteous life produce a certain level of confidence? Yes. But it is not enough to make you bold as a lion. As the Old Testament book of Daniel puts it, "the people who know their God shall be strong, and carry out great exploits."[17] The boldness that characterizes a lionhearted life comes from confidence in knowing God. When you shore that up, your roar will come out.

Uncaged

One of the most unnatural sights is a caged lion. Even when you are walking through a zoo, the sight of captive big cats is inherently disappointing. Yes, it feels safe, but it also feels absurd. This is why a safari is more satisfying than a trip to your local zoo. You are seeing wild animals in their natural element. It is so much more awe-inspiring to observe lions inhabit a space they were meant for than to watch them pace back and forth or sleep behind plexiglass. A domesticated lion is a contradiction in terms. This is why, though sad, it is never shocking when you hear of someone getting mauled to death by their pet lion. They weren't created for cages. This reality signals why life feels like so much less than it's meant to be when men have allowed the dictates of culture, the pressure of peers, the need to impress, and the standards of society to define the borders of their life. They have been caged. The borders of their lives have been drawn by what was never intended to dictate their destiny.

The reason this observation is so poignant is that this is the issue Solomon speaks to directly in Proverbs 4:23: "Guard your heart above all else, for it determines the course of your life" (NLT). The Hebrew word translated "determines the course" is *totsaah-owt*. It was term used at times in relation to cartography.[18] Think mapmaking, determining boundaries, city limits, and marking borders. Solomon's use of this word creates a trail of breadcrumbs leading to a massive truth. The heart is not just the genesis point of your life; it also determines the limits of your life. It sets the boundaries and borders of your life. The point is, if you want to know where your life is going, look at where your heart is going. In the same way, what you allow to confine and define your existence at the heart level will draw the boundary lines of your life. You can be caged by fear, bitterness, anxiety, people's opinions, personal pain, or cultural pushback, and those will become the border walls which will inevitably define your existence. You will shrink back from opportunities. You will avoid stepping into situations that may bring conflict. You will erect barriers in relationships that require transparency. This is why the core of who you are matters so much. Your heart is the one thing that determines everything.

He Isn't Safe

The purpose of the journey through these chapters has not only been to give you insight into yourself but also to open your eyes to things you didn't even realize were holding you back. Everyone has something. Yet only the original lion, the prototype for the lionhearted man, Jesus Christ, can give you a picture of what the lionhearted life looks like and empower you to destroy the barriers that boxed you in. It's no great surprise that one of our favorite allegorical pictures of Jesus is Aslan from C. S. Lewis's classic *The Lion, the Witch and the Wardrobe* from his series The Chronicles of Narnia. As the children who have entered Narnia are orienting themselves to this land's otherworldly realities, they start asking Mr. Beaver (who is an actual beaver, by the way) about Aslan.

> "Is—is he a man?" asked Lucy.
>
> "Aslan a man!" said Mr. Beaver sternly, "Certainly not . . . Aslan is a lion—*the* Lion, the great Lion."
>
> "Ooh!" said Susan. "I'd thought he was a man. Is he— quite safe? I shall feel rather nervous about meeting a lion."
>
> "Safe?" said Mr. Beaver, "Who said anything about safe? 'Course he isn't safe. But he's good. He's the King, I tell you."[19]

The Lion of the tribe of Judah isn't safe. We're not talking about a domesticated house cat. He is ferocious. He is awesome. He is not a tame lion. And in His incarnate humanity, He gave us a picture of the lionhearted life. A life that was characterized by grace and truth, humility and wholehearted devotion, suffering and strength. The life that Proverbs points every man toward. It's the lionhearted way of living that you have been called and empowered to emulate. It flows from the Christ-bought, God-given, Spirit-indwelt heart you have been given.

You have what you need.

The lionhearted life is yours for the living.

No more excuses.

You are done shrinking back.

You are ready to roar.

CONCLUSION

Do not despise these small beginnings, for
the LORD rejoices to see the work begin.
Zechariah 4:10 NLT

From a small seed a mighty trunk may grow.
Aeschylus

In the heart of Sequoia National Park is a tree that has been around since before Jesus walked this earth. It goes by the name General Sherman, and it's the largest tree in the world. Each year, the tree's growth adds enough new wood to build an entire house! We have no doubt that you probably already knew all of that, because you are very smart, but do you know the name of the world's second largest tree?

Located just twenty-nine miles away, just inside Kings Canyon National Park, the General Grant tree receives far fewer visitors than the more than two million who flock

215

to see General Sherman. But it is also a giant sequoia, and though it's nearly six thousand cubic feet smaller than General Sherman and 350 years younger, it is still a massively impressive tree. Even if you were familiar with General Sherman, the General Grant tree is probably not on your radar because it's not the largest. It's definitely not small, but in a way, you could say it's in the process of becoming like its older brother.

When something is "in process," it can feel insignificant or at least less significant than it actually is. This is especially true if it's being viewed in comparison with something bigger, more mature, or further along; its progress can garner a lot less fanfare. The reality of its growth or size may even be received with a yawn to the casual observer. Additionally, if you were to road-trip to Kings Canyon National Park for an afternoon of staring at General Grant, you might conclude that no growth is taking place at all, but you would be wrong.

When something is in process, its progress can be hard to observe. It can even be easy to despise the growth that has taken place if it's constantly being compared with something else. The same thing can happen in our evaluation of our own hearts.

While Jesus has saved us, and in doing so gave us new hearts, the evidence of that new heart and the personal growth taking place can at times seem slow or imperceptible. This can lead to discouragement and, if you're not careful, you can sabotage the progress, causing you to mistakenly believe that the lionhearted life is outside of your reach. Perhaps as you have read this book, you have found yourself taking two steps forward and one step back. Maybe while you were reading this book, you felt the Spirit of God, prayed, and heard God's voice, only to find yourself now feeling you are back at square one. Be encouraged: whether you see it or feel it, you *are* growing. You are becoming lionhearted. The fact that you made it to this page bears witness to that fact!

God is doing a deep work on the inside of you, and you are not always instantaneously aware of how He has changed you or is changing you. Everyone likes when things are instant, but just like those giant, majestic, stunning sequoias, heart work takes time. But it's worth it. God sees you as significant, and what He is doing in you is significant.

We both like planting trees. Our wives find it humorous and sometimes annoying that if we go to the hardware store, we usually return home with something new to plant. But our amateur arborist logic is the sooner you plant them, the sooner you get to enjoy their growth! Professional arborists will tell you that when you plant a tree, the first year they sleep, the second year they creep, and the third year they leap. That means much care, effort, mulch, water, sunlight, and fertilizer will all be given to that tree without initially seeing results, but things are happening. Roots are going deep.

We know, with Jesus's help, you are becoming a lionhearted man. You will be focused, fulfilled, and fearless because He who began a good work in you will bring it to completion. So be strong and courageous. Guard your heart, live life on purpose, never quit, and definitely don't settle. And remember, "Do not despise these small beginnings, for the LORD rejoices to see the work begin."[1]

ACKNOWLEDGMENTS

Our families: As any author knows, writing a book takes enormous amounts of time and energy. Our wives and kids cheered us on through the entire journey, even when that meant we were lost in thought. We are so thankful for their prayers and support.

Our parents: Our dad and mom have both written books, and we are thankful for the opportunity to follow in their steps. They were excited about this project from the moment we told them the idea, and we are so grateful for their faith-filled leadership and legacy.

Our church: Getting to be part of any church is a gift, but we count ourselves over-the-top blessed to be part of what God is doing through James River Church. We can't express how thankful we are for the privilege of serving such amazing people.

Our crew: Writing something worth reading never happens without people who are willing to partner with you in the process, and we had a team of incredible people who were willing to read drafts, help with research, and check our grammar. Thank you, Becky Davis, Cathi Keene, Kaysie Uhrig, Katrina Weidknecht, and Kylie Box. We also have the privilege of working with some incredibly creative designers and photographers. Thank you, Nathanael Burks, Josiah Hartmann, and Jared Lung. Additionally, we want to give a big shout-out to Jonathan Martin, who is always so generous with his time and creative energy. Finally, this project would not have happened without the wise counsel of Randal Taylor.

Our publisher: The team at Baker is off the charts! They were a huge gift to us. We were especially grateful for the opportunity to work with our editor, Andrea Doering.

Our Savior: We know it can feel cliché for Christian authors to thank God, but it shouldn't. We would have nothing to say apart from Him leading us into truth through His Word and the guiding hand of the Holy Spirit. He gets the glory for anything you get out of these pages.

NOTES

Chapter 1 Most Wanted

1. "The comparative, *above every (mikkol-)* constitutes the standard by which the quality of guarding the heart is measured (i.e., it must be reckoned as more important than anything else that one needs to restrain)." Bruce K. Waltke, *The Book of Proverbs, Chapters 1–15*, The New International Commentary on the Old Testament (Grand Rapids: Eerdmans, 2004), 297.

2. Rick Warren, *The Purpose Driven Life: What On Earth Am I Here For?* (Grand Rapids: Zondervan, 2012), Apple Books.

3. Daniel Cox, Beatrice Lee, and Dana Popky, "How Prevalent is Pornography?," Institute For Family Studies, May 3, 2022, https://ifstudies.org/blog/how-prevalent-is-pornography.

4. Serah Louis, "'The Most Chilling Metric of All': Mike Rowe Warns That 7 Million American Men Are 'Done' Looking for Work and Have 'Punched Out'—Why That's a Serious Problem," Yahoo Finance, March 19, 2023, https://finance.yahoo.com/news/most-chilling-metric-mike-rowe-150000193.html?guccounter=1.

5. Matthew F. Garnett and Sally C. Curtin, "Suicide Mortality in the United States, 2001–2021," NCHS Data Brief no. 464 (April 2023), https://www.cdc.gov/nchs/products/databriefs/db464.htm.

6. Richard V. Reeves, *Of Boys and Men: Why the Modern Male Is Struggling, Why It Matters, and What to Do About It* (Washington, DC: Brookings Institution Press, 2022), Apple Books.

7. Barrett Swanson, "Men at Work: Is There a Masculine Cure for Toxic Masculinity?," *Harper's Magazine*, November 2019, https://harpers.org/archive/2019/11/men-at-work-evryman-barrett-swanson/.

8. Matt. 15:19 NLT.

9. John Maxwell, *Failing Forward: Turning Mistakes into Stepping Stones to Success* (New York: HarperCollins Leadership, 2000), Apple Books.

Chapter 2 Hell in Your Heart

1. NPR, "The Al-Qaida 'Triple Agent' Who Infiltrated the CIA," July 19, 2011, https://www.npr.org/2011/07/19/138158669/the-al-qaida-triple-agent-who-infiltrated-the-cia.

2. Phil Stewart, "CIA Acknowledges 'Missteps' Led to Officers' Deaths," Reuters, October 20, 2010, https://www.reuters.com/article/us-usa-cia-bombing/cia-acknowledges-missteps-led-to-officers-deaths-idUSTRE69J04720101020.

3. NPR, "The Al-Qaida 'Triple Agent.'"

4. John Flavel, *Keeping the Heart: Lessons on Maintaining a Pure Heart in All Seasons of Life*, ed. Jon D. Fogdall (Abbotsford, WI: Aneko Press, 2022), Apple Books.

5. Mark 7:21 ESV.

6. Sally C. Curtin, Matthew F. Garnett, and Farida B. Ahmad, "Provisional Numbers and Rates of Suicide by Month and Demographic Characteristics: United States, 2021," NCHS Vital Statistics Rapid Release Report 24 (September 2022), https://stacks.cdc.gov/view/cdc/120830; "Long-Term Trends in Depths of Despair," United States Congress Joint Economic Committee, September 5, 2019, https://www.jec.senate.gov/public/index.cfm/republicans/2019/9/long-term-trends-in-deaths-of-despair; Patrick T. Brown, "Opioids and the Unattached Male," Ethics & Public Policy Center, January 14, 2022, https://eppc.org/publication/opioids-and-the-unattached-male/.

7. Karol Lewczuk, Adrian Wojcik, and Mateusz Gola, "Increase in the Prevalence of Online Pornography Use: Objective Data Analysis from the Period Between 2004 and 2016 in Poland," *Archives of Sexual Behavior* 51, no. 2 (February 2022), https://doi.org/10.1007/s10508-021-02090-w.

8. "Top 100: The Most Visited Websites in the US [2022 Top Websites Edition]," *Semrush* (blog), accessed March 8, 2023, https://www.semrush.com/blog/most-visited-websites/.

9. Stephanie Kramer, "U.S. Has World's Highest Rate of Children Living in Single-Parent Households," Pew Research Center, December 12, 2019, https://www.pewresearch.org/short-reads/2019/12/12/u-s-children-more-likely-than-children-in-other-countries-to-live-with-just-one-parent/.

10. Daniel A. Cox, Beatrice Lee, and Dana Popky, "Politics, Sex, and Sexuality: The Growing Gender Divide in American Life," Survey Center on American Life, April 27, 2022, https://www.americansurveycenter.org/research/march-2022-aps/.

11. Neil Postman, *Amusing Ourselves to Death: Public Discourse in the Age of Show Business* (New York: Penguin Books, 2005), chapter 11, Apple Books.

12. Josh Hawley, *Manhood: The Masculine Virtues America Needs* (Washington, DC: Regnery, 2023), 7.

13. Friedrich Nietzsche, *Thus Spoke Zarathustra (A Modernized Translation with a New Introduction and Biography)*, ed. Bill Chapko (2010), Kindle.

14. John Owen, *Temptation and Sin*, vol. 6, *The Works of John Owen*, ed. William H. Goold (Edinburgh: T&T Clark, 1991), 9.

15. Gen. 1:31.

16. Gen. 2:16–17 NLT.

17. Gen. 3:4–5 NLT.

18. R. C. Sproul, *Essential Truths of the Christian Faith* (Carol Stream, IL: Tyndale House Publishers, 1992), 180.

19. Jer. 17:9 NKJV.

20. Erwin W. Lutzer, *God's Devil: The Incredible Story of How Satan's Rebellion Serves God's Purposes* (Chicago: Moody Publishers, 2015), 52.

21. James 3:15.

22. Warren W. Wiersbe, *The Bible Exposition Commentary*, vol. 2 (Wheaton: Victor Books, 1996), 363. Wiersbe writes,

> But this "wisdom that is from beneath" is also "devilish." Perhaps the best translation is *demonic*. Beginning with Genesis 3, where Satan successfully deceived Eve, and continuing through the entire Bible, there is a "wisdom of Satan" at work, fighting against the wisdom of God. Satan convinced Eve that she would be like God. He told her that the tree would make her wise. Ever since that event, people have continued to believe Satan's lies and have tried to become their own gods (Rom. 1:18–25). Satan

is cunning; he is the old serpent! He has wisdom that will confound and confuse you if you do not know the wisdom of God.

23. Rom. 7:21 NLT.

24. Jer. 17:9 NLT.

Chapter 3 Getting the Hell Out of Your Heart

1. James C. Cobb, "What We Learn From Coca-Cola's Biggest Blunder," *Time*, July 10, 2015, https://time.com/3950205/new-coke-history-america/.

2. Christopher Klein, "Why Coca-Cola's New Coke Flopped," History, September 14, 2023, https://www.history.com/news/why-coca-cola-new-coke-flopped#.

3. Lawrence K. Altman, "Norman E. Shumway, 83, Who Made the Heart Transplant a Standard," *New York Times*, February 11, 2006, https://www.nytimes.com/2006/02/11/health/norman-e-shumway-83-who-made-the-heart-transplant-a-standard.html.

4. Steve Maraboli, "The Quote Archive," Tiny Buddha, accessed January 15, 2024, https://tinybuddha.com/wisdom-quotes/stop-trying-fix-youre-not-broken-perfectly-imperfect-powerful-beyond-measure/.

5. Ezek. 36:26.

6. Heb. 3:7–8 NLT.

7. Charles Spurgeon, *The Stony Heart Removed*, vol. 8, *The Metropolitan Tabernacle Pulpit Sermons* (London: Passmore & Alabaster, 1862), 357.

8. Pfeiffer writes, "The reminder of Israel's sin in wilderness days serves as a warning to those waiting to enter the Temple." Charles F. Pfeiffer, *The Wycliffe Bible Commentary: Old Testament* (Chicago: Moody Press, 1962), Ps. 95:8.

9. Matt. 11:12 ESV. "Both 11:12a and 11:12b should be understood as positive statements about the advance of the kingdom (NIV). The verb βιάζεται is interpreted as a middle voice reflecting the dynamic advance of God's rule (12:28). The forceful grabbing of the kingdom in 11:12b is viewed as enthusiastic converts pressing into the kingdom (Calvin 1972: 2.7; Hendriksen 1973: 488–90; Keener 1999: 339–40). This approach was popular among Greek patristic sources (e.g., Clement of Alexandria, Paed. 3.7.39; Irenaeus, Haer. 4.37.7)." David L. Turner, *Matthew*, Baker Exegetical Commentary on the New Testament (Grand Rapids: Baker Academic, 2008), 294.

10. John Piper, "How Can I Soften My Own Heart?," Desiring God, September 9, 2016, https://www.desiringgod.org/interviews/how-can-i-soften-my-own-heart.

Chapter 4 The Inner Life of a Lion

1. Al Pearce, "How Richard Petty's First Career NASCAR Win Came Thanks to Dad Lee (And Rex White)," *Autoweek*, February 5, 2024, https://www.autoweek.com/racing/nascar/a46651669/richard-petty-first-career-nascar-win/.

2. Jesse Kiser, "The King's First Elephant," *MotorTrend*, March 21, 2024, https://www.motortrend.com/news/the-kings-first-elephant/.

3. Prov. 4:23.

4. Robert Saucy, *Minding the Heart: The Way of Spiritual Transformation* (Grand Rapids: Kregel, 2013), 115.

5. Eph. 2:8.

6. Anthony A. Hoekema, *Created in God's Image* (Grand Rapids: Eerdmans, 1994), 83–84. "Because of the Fall, therefore, the image of God in man, though not destroyed, has been seriously corrupted. Calvin, it will be recalled, described this image as deformed, vitiated, mutilated, maimed, disease-ridden, and disfigured. Herman Bavinck at one time even used the word *devastated* (*verwoestte*) to depict what sin has done to the image of God in man (though he would not deny that fallen man still retains the image of God in a sense)."

7. As we have argued throughout the book, not only is God the one who gives a person a new heart, but it is the Holy Spirit who continues to empower the way of life that God has made possible through the gift of a new heart.

8. Dane Ortlund, *Gentle and Lowly: The Heart of Christ for Sinners and Sufferers* (Wheaton: Crossway, 2020), 18.

9. Hans Walter Wolff, *Anthropology of the Old Testament* (London: SCM Press, 2012), 40.

10. Saucy, *Minding the Heart*, 31.

11. There are 156 references to the "heart" (*kardia*) in the New Testament. Saucy, *Minding the Heart*, 34.

12. Gen. 2:7 NLT.

13. Saucy, *Minding the Heart*, 32–33.

14. Deut. 29:4 ESV.

15. Heb. 4:12.

16. "Crooked Teeth," track 2 on Death Cab for Cutie, *Plans*. Atlantic Records, 2005, compact disc.

17. John 14:1.

18. Isa. 65:14 ESV.

19. Ps. 21:2.

20. Acts 11:23 NASB.

21. 1 Cor. 4:5 NASB 1995.

22. Ortlund, *Gentle and Lowly*, 18.

23. John Flavel, *Keeping the Heart: Lessons on Maintaining a Pure Heart in All Seasons of Life*, ed. Jon D. Fogdall (Abbotsford, WI: Aneko Press, 2022), Apple Books.

24. 1 Pet. 2:2.

25. 1 Kings 3:9 MSG.

Chapter 5 The He(ART) of Self-Deception

1. Leslie Maitland, "At the Heart of the Abscam Debate," *New York Times*, July 25, 1982, https://www.nytimes.com/1982/07/25/magazine/at-the-heart-of-the-abscam-debate.html.

2. Leslie Maitland, "Mel Weinberg: The Conman Who Flipped," *Politico Magazine*, December 30, 2018, https://www.politico.com/magazine/story/2018/12/30/mel-weinberg-the-conman-who-flipped-223414/.

3. Ps. 139:23–24 NLT.

4. Richard P. Feynman, "Cargo Cult Science," *Engineering and Science* 37, no. 7 (1974), http://calteches.library.caltech.edu/51/2/CargoCult.htm.

5. John Owen, *Temptation and Sin*, vol. 6, *The Works of John Owen*, ed. William H. Goold (Edinburgh: T&T Clark, 1991), 56.

6. George Saunders, *Liberation Day: Stories* (New York: Random House, 2022), Kindle.

7. Robert Saucy, *Minding the Heart: The Way of Spiritual Transformation* (Grand Rapids: Kregel, 2013), 83.

8. Perkin Amalaraj, "Ukrainian Sniper Claims New World Record after 'Picking Off Russian Soldier from 2.36 Miles Away Using "Lord of the Horizon" Gun,'" *Daily Mail*, November 20, 2023, https://www.dailymail.co.uk/news/article-12770127/Ukrainian-sniper-claims-new-world-record-picking-Russian-soldier-2-36-miles-away-using-Lord-Horizon-gun.html.

9. Leonard Ravenhill, "AZ Quotes," accessed April 4, 2024, https://www.azquotes.com/ quote/718830.

10. Obad. 1:3.

11. See 1 Sam. 13:8–15.

12. 1 Sam. 14:24–48.

13. Phil. 2:12–13.

14. Said in personal conversation, February 17, 2022.

15. John Flavel, *Keeping the Heart: Lessons on Maintaining a Pure Heart in All Seasons of Life*, ed. Jon D. Fogdall (Abbotsford, WI: Aneko Press, 2022), Apple Books.

16. Ps. 139:24 MSG.

Chapter 6 The Heist from Hell

1. Ben Johnson, "The Theft of the Crown Jewels," Historic UK, https://www.historic-uk.com/HistoryUK/HistoryofEngland/The-Theft-of-the-Crown-Jewels/.

2. Prov. 4:23.

3. Wayne Grudem, "Keep Your Heart with All Vigilance: Proverbs 4:23," August 17, 2022, https://www.youtube.com/watch?v=rDnfyZxb9O0.

4. William David Reyburn and Euan McG. Fry, *A Handbook on Proverbs*, UBS Handbook Series (New York: United Bible Societies, 2000), 112.

5. Erwin W. Lutzer, *God's Devil: The Incredible Story of How Satan's Rebellion Served God's Purposes* (Chicago: Moody Publishers, 2015), 145. The book you are reading provides a very limited treatment of the devil, so if you are interested in learning more about what Scripture says about the devil, I would highly recommend this little book by Lutzer.

6. 1 Pet. 5:8 NLT.

7. Warren W. Wiersbe, *Ephesians–Revelation*, vol. 2, *The Bible Exposition Commentary* (Wheaton: Victor Books, 1996), 432.

8. Karen H. Jobes, *1 Peter*, Baker Exegetical Commentary on the New Testament (Grand Rapids: Baker Academic, 2005), 314.

9. Job 1:7.

10. William Thomas Ellis, *Billy Sunday, the Man and His Message: With His Own Words which Have Won Thousands for Christ* (Philadelphia: John C. Winston Company, 1917), 79.

11. Henry George Liddell and Robert Scott, *A Greek-English Lexicon*, s.v. "καταπίνω" (Oxford: Clarendon Press, 1996), 905.

12. Stephen J. Sansweet, *Star Wars Encyclopedia*, s.v. "sarlacc" (New York: Del Rey, 1998), 258.

13. Acts 5:3 NLT.

14. 1 Pet. 5:9.

15. Thomas R. Schreiner, *1, 2 Peter, Jude,* vol. 37, *The New American Commentary* (Nashville: Broadman & Holman Publishers, 2003), 242.

16. Eph. 6:10–13.

17. John Flavel, *Keeping the Heart: Lessons on Maintaining a Pure Heart in All Seasons of Life*, ed. Jon D. Fogdall (Abbotsford, WI: Aneko Press, 2022), Apple Books.

18. Eph. 6:10.

19. Eph. 3:16 ESV.

20. Eph. 6:13.

21. Eph. 6:14.

22. Phil. 3:7–9.

23. Phil. 2:12–13 NLT. "Dear friends, you always followed my instructions when I was with you. And now that I am away, it is even more important. Work hard to show the results of your salvation, obeying God with deep reverence and fear. For God is working in you, giving you the desire and the power to do what pleases him."

24. Eph. 6:15.

25. R. Kent Hughes, *Ephesians: The Mystery of the Body of Christ*, Preaching the Word (Wheaton: Crossway Books, 1990), 232.

26. Eph. 6:17.

27. 1 John 2:14.

28. James 4:7.

Chapter 7 The Jaws of Life (and Death)

1. "What Are Jaws of Life?," Fenton Fire, accessed September 20, 2024, https://www.fentonfire.com/blog/jaws-of-life/.

2. Matt Fratus, "'3 Minutes to Save a Life': The Man Responsible for the Jaws of Life," *Coffee or Die Magazine*, May 10, 2021, https://coffeeordie.com/george-hurst-jaws-of-life.

3. "The Jaws of Life Story," Frohlich Gordon Beason Injury Law, accessed September 20, 2024, https://fgblawfirm.com/the-jaws-of-life-story/.

4. Jim Donnelly, "George Hurst," *Hemmings*, September 23, 2018, https://www.hemmings.com/stories/george-hurst/.

5. "The Jaws of Life: A Quick Overview," *Daniel Stark Injury Lawyers* (blog), September 29, 2022, https://www.danielstark.com/blog/the-jaws-of-life-a-quick-overview/.

6. "Saved from the Jaws of Death by the Jaws of Life: A Love of Telling Stories + a Penchant for Preserving History + Social Media + a Father's Legacy = A Quite Unexpected Journey," *Mickey Herr* (blog), March 13,

2014, https://mickeyherr.com/2014/03/23/saved-from-the-jaws-of-death
-by-the-jaws-of-life-a-love-of-telling-stories-a-penchant-for-preserving
-history-social-media-a-fathers-legacy-a-quite-unexpected-journey/.

7. "Jaws of Life," *Daniel Stark*.

8. John 1:29.

9. Rev. 5:5.

10. Prov. 18:21 MSG.

11. Matt. 12:37.

12. Matt. 16:23.

13. James 3:3–6 ESV.

14. James 3:5 ESV.

15. James 3:6 ESV.

16. Prov. 12:18 ESV.

17. James 3:6 ESV.

18. James 3:8 ESV.

19. Augustine of Hippo, *Four Anti-Pelagian Writings*, ed. Thomas P. Halton, trans. John A. Mourant and William J. Collinge, vol. 86, The Fathers of the Church (Washington, DC: Catholic University of America Press, 1992), 33.

20. James 3:9 ESV.

21. Gen. 1:26 ESV.

22. Matt. 15:11, 18 ESV.

23. James 3:11–12.

24. Matt. 12:34–35 ESV.

25. Matt. 21:21.

26. Prov. 18:21.

27. Gen. 1:3.

28. Prov. 18:21 MSG.

29. Ps. 139:23 ESV.

30. Jer. 17:9 NKJV.

31. Matt. 12:34 ESV.

Chapter 8 The Eyes of a Lion

1. Ryan Erik King, "Both Pilots Fall Asleep During Flight, Co-Pilot Blames Tiredness On His Newborn Twins," Yahoo, March 11, 2024, https://autos.yahoo.com/both-pilots-fall-asleep-during-193941490.html; Rebecca Cohen, "Indonesian Flight Veered Off Course after Both Pilots Allegedly Fell Asleep in the Cockpit," NBC News, March 10, 2024, https://www.nbcnews.com/news/world

/indonesian-flight-veered-course-both-pilots-allegedly-fell-asleep
-cock-rcna142683.

2. Prov. 4:25 NLT.

3. Bruce K. Waltke, *The Book of Proverbs, Chapters 1–15*, The New International Commentary on the Old Testament (Grand Rapids: Eerdmans, 2004), 300.

4. Duane A. Garrett, *Proverbs, Ecclesiastes, Song of Songs*, vol. 14, *The New American Commentary* (Nashville: Broadman & Holman Publishers, 1993), 89.

5. Aldous Huxley, *Brave New World Revisited* (New York: RosettaBooks, 2010), Kindle.

6. "People Touch Their Smartphone Over 2,600 Times a Day, Research Shows," *Brussels Times*, June 3, 2022, https://www.brussels times.com/232851/people-touch-their-smartphone-over-2600-times -a-day-research-shows.

7. L'Oreal Thompson Payton, "Americans Check Their Phones 144 Times a Day. Here's How to Cut Back," Fortune Well, July 19, 2023, https://fortune.com/well/2023/07/19/how-to-cut-back-screen-time/.

8. Neil Postman, *Amusing Ourselves to Death: Public Discourse in the Age of Show Business* (New York: Penguin Books, 1986), Apple Books.

9. Eccles. 1:8 NLT.

10. Daphne LePrince-Ringuet, "Here's Scientific Proof Your Brain Was Designed to Be Distracted," Wired, August 22, 2018, https://www .wired.com/story/brain-distraction-procrastination-science/.

11. Matt. 6:22–23.

12. Reena Mukamal, "Early Signs of Heart Disease Appear in the Eyes," American Academy of Ophthalmology, April 27, 2022, https:// www.aao.org/eye-health/news/eye-stroke-heart-disease-vision-exam -retina-oct.

13. Charles Spurgeon, "Sermon: The King and His Court," Spurgeon Gems, accessed March 21, 2024, http://www.spurgeongems.org /sermon/chs2362.pdf.

14. Adrian Rogers, "The Poison of Pornography," OnePlace, accessed March 24, 2024, https://www.oneplace.com/ministries/love -worth-finding/read/articles/the-poison-of-pornography-15292.html.

15. Francis Brown, S. R. Driver, and Charles A. Briggs, *The Brown-Driver-Briggs Hebrew and English Lexicon* (Peabody, MA: Hendrickson Publishers, 1996), 116.

16. Job 31:1 NLT.

17. Movies get made to make money, and as the viewer, you are the one funding every scene. A lionhearted man should determine to never be part of the reason the studio decided it was a good business decision to make a film that includes sexually explicit content.

18. Ps. 119:37 ESV.

19. "Lion," Southland Eye, accessed May 6, 2024, https://southland eye.com/lion/.

20. Andres Valdes, "What Leaders Can Learn from Lions About Vision," Andres Valdes, accessed May 6, 2024, https://andresvaldes .com/what-leaders-can-learn-from-lions-about-vision/.

21. Eph. 1:18 ESV.

22. John 1:5 NLT.

23. 2 Cor. 4:6.

24. Murray J. Harris, *The Second Epistle to the Corinthians*, New International Greek Testament Commentary (Grand Rapids: Eerdmans, 2005), 335. The New Testament theologian Murray Harris wrote, "Not only is the agent the same; the result of the action is the same—the creation and diffusion of light and consequently the dispersing and dispelling of darkness."

25. Ps. 139:12 ESV.

26. Ps. 11:3 ESV.

Chapter 9 Where Lions Tread

1. Taryn Asher, "Detroit Police Officers Fight Each Other in Undercover Op Gone Wrong," Fox 2 Detroit, November 13, 2017, https:// www.fox2detroit.com/news/detroit-police-officers-fight-each-other -in-undercover-op-gone-wrong.

2. Martin Belam, "Detroit Police Officers Brawl After Undercover Drugs Raid Goes Wrong," *Guardian*, November 17, 2017, https:// www.theguardian.com/us-news/2017/nov/17/detroit-police-officers -brawl-after-undercover-drugs-raid-goes-wrong.

3. Ps. 1:1.

4. Timothy J. Keller, "The Search for Happiness," September 12, 1993, *The Timothy Keller Sermon Archive 1989–2011* (New York City: Redeemer Presbyterian Church, 2013).

5. Prov. 4:26 ESV.

6. Ps. 1:1.

7. Charles Spurgeon, *The Treasury of David: Psalms 1–26*, vol. 1 (London: Marshall Brothers, n.d.), 1–2.

8. Prov. 13:20 ESV.

9. Robert Frost, "The Road Not Taken," in *Major American Writers*, vol. 2, ed. Howard Mumford Jones, Ernest E. Leisy, and Richard M. Ludwig (New York: Harcourt, Brace, 1952), 1609.

10. Jay Perini, "Listening for God in Unusual Places: The Unorthodox Faith of Robert Frost," *America Magazine*, February 20, 2013, https://www.americamagazine.org/issue/listening-god-unusual -places.

11. Matt. 7:13–14.

12. John Bunyan, *The Pilgrim's Progress*, vol. 3, *The Works of John Bunyan* (Bellingham, WA: Logos Bible Software, 2006), 98.

13. Ps. 84:5 ESV.

Chapter 10 THE Lionhearted Man

1. J. Mark Powell, "Holy Cow! History: The Man Who Sold The Eiffel Tower," My Journal Courier, August 14, 2022, https://www .myjournalcourier.com/news/article/Holy-cow-History-The-man -who-sold-the-Eiffel-17367737.php.

2. Jeff Maysh, "The Man Who Sold the Eiffel Tower. Twice," *Smithsonian Magazine*, March 9, 2016, https://www.smithsonianmag .com/history/man-who-sold-eiffel-tower-twice-180958370/.

3. 1 Cor. 13:9.

4. Tremper Longman III, *Proverbs*, vol. 2, *Baker Commentary on the Old Testament Wisdom and Psalms* (Grand Rapids: Baker Academic, 2006), 67.

5. Augustine, *Tractates on the Gospel of John*, vol. 7 of Nicene and Post-Nicene Fathers, First Series, trans. John Gibb, ed. Philip Schaff (Buffalo, New York: Christian Literature Publishing, 1888), 9.5.

6. Longman III, *Proverbs*, 66.

7. 1 Cor. 1:30 NLT.

8. Luke 24:25, 27 NLT.

9. Acts 10:38 ESV.

10. Luke 10:27.

11. Matt. 3:17 NKJV.

12. John 5:19.

13. Luke 4:18–19.

14. C. S. Lewis, *The Weight of Glory* (New York: Macmillan, 1949), 1–3. © 1949 CS Lewis Pte Ltd. Extract used with permission.

15. John 1:14.

16. John 8:10.
17. Matt. 9:13.
18. John 4:32.
19. Ps. 23:5.

Chapter 11 The Carnivore Diet

1. Arielle Tschinkel, "Someone Called 911 Because Their Chicken Nuggets Weren't Ready Fast Enough," Yahoo! Life, June 15, 2017, https://www.yahoo.com/lifestyle/someone-called-911-because-chicken-170643087.html.

2. Tamara Willner, "Can't Stop Eating Junk Food? Here's Why," Second Nature, updated July 2024, https://www.secondnature.io/us/guides/nutrition/cant-stop-eating-junk-food#.

3. "Decoding Cravings: Why Your Body Craves Junk Food," Doctors Hospital, November 9, 2020, https://doctors-hospital.net/blog/entry/decoding-cravings-why-your-body-craves-junk-food.

4. John 4:34 ESV.

5. Ps. 34:8.

6. "Lions: Kruger Park Wildlife Facts," Siyabona Africa, accessed May 20, 2024, https://www.krugerpark.co.za/Kruger_National_Park_Wildlife-travel/kruger-park-wildlife-lions.html.

7. Matt. 4:4.

8. Matt. 4:4.

9. Matt. 4:2.

10. John Nolland, *The Gospel of Matthew*, The New International Greek Testament Commentary (Grand Rapids: Eerdmans, 2005), 164.

11. "Why Europa," Europa Clipper, accessed May 9, 2024, https://europa.nasa.gov/why-europa/ingredients-for-life/.

12. Highlands College, "Pray First | Pastor Chris Hodges," 52:30, January 17, 2023, https://www.youtube.com/watch?v=aNlr7gUD9U8.

13. John 4:34 ESV.

14. St. Augustine, *Homilies on the Gospel according to St. John, and His First Epistle*, vol. 1 & 2, A Library of Fathers of the Holy Catholic Church (Oxford: John Henry Parker, 1848), 247.

15. Douglas Wilson, "The Marks of a Pharisee," Blog & Mablog, November 20, 2005, https://dougwils.com/the-church/practical-christianity/the-marks-of-a-pharisee.html.

16. Luke 5:16.

17. John Flavel, *Keeping the Heart: Lessons on Maintaining a Pure Heart in All Seasons of Life*, ed. Jon D. Fogdall (Abbotsford, WI: Aneko Press, 2022), Apple Books.

18. J. C. Ryle, *Thoughts For Young Men* (Johannesburg: Primedia, 2011), Apple Books.

19. James Swanson, *Dictionary of Biblical Languages with Semantic Domains: Greek (New Testament)*, s.v. "ἔρημος," (Bellingham, WA: Faithlife, 1997).

20. Prov. 27:17; 17:17.

21. John Piper, "God Is the Gospel, Session 2," Desiring God, October 21, 2006, https://www.desiringgod.org/messages/god-is-the-gospel-session-2.

22. Virginia Woolf, *A Room of One's Own* (New York: Harcourt, 1929), Apple Books.

23. 2 Pet. 1:3.

Chapter 12 Ready to Roar

1. A. Brad Schwartz, "The Infamous 'War of the Worlds' Radio Broadcast Was a Magnificent Fluke," *Smithsonian Magazine*, May 6, 2015, https://www.smithsonianmag.com/history/infamous-war-worlds-radio-broadcast-was-magnificent-fluke-180955180/.

2. Michael Reeves, ed., *Rejoice and Tremble: The Surprising Good News of the Fear of the Lord* (Wheaton: Crossway, 2021), 28.

3. Henry David Thoreau, *Walden* (Glendale, WI: Global Publishers, 2022), Kindle.

4. Prov. 9:10.

5. James 2:19.

6. Gen. 3:10.

7. Reeves, *Rejoice and Tremble*, 31.

8. Jer. 32:40 ESV.

9. Isa. 8:12–13 ESV.

10. John Bunyan, *The Holy War*, vol. 3 (Bellingham, WA: Logos Bible Software, 2006), 351.

11. Isa. 53:3 ESV.

12. 1 Pet. 5:8 NLT.

13. Warren W. Wiersbe, *The Bible Exposition Commentary*, vol. 2 (Wheaton: Victor Books, 1996), 433.

14. Matt. 11:12 ESV.

15. Craig S. Keener, *Matthew*, vol. 1, *The IVP New Testament Commentary Series* (Downers Grove, IL: InterVarsity, 1997), Matt.

11:12–15. There is scholarly debate around the meaning of Jesus's words, but we are inclined to agree with Craig Keener's reading of this text. Keener writes, "The Kingdom Belongs to Those Who Contend for It . . . Compare Luke 16:16. Our roles may be determined by grace, but grace does not erase human responsibility."

16. A. W. Tozer, *The Knowledge of the Holy* (New York: HarperCollins, 1978), 1.

17. Dan. 11:32 NKJV.

18. William Lee Holladay and Ludwig Köhler, *A Concise Hebrew and Aramaic Lexicon of the Old Testament* (Leiden: Brill, 2000), 388.

19. C. S. Lewis, *The Lion, the Witch and the Wardrobe* (New York: Harper Trophy, 1950), 86. © 1950 C.S. Lewis Pte. Ltd. Extract reprinted by permission.

Conclusion

1. Zech. 4:10 NLT.

DAVID LINDELL serves as a pastor at James River Church. He is passionate about developing leaders, championing the local church, and teaching the Bible. He and his wife, Becky, have four children. He has a ThM from Dallas Theological Seminary.

BRANDON LINDELL serves as the executive ministry pastor at James River Church. From worship to design to video to production and more, he inspires people to follow Jesus wholeheartedly. He and his wife, Beth, have four children.

Dear Reader,

Thank you for selecting a Revell book! We're so happy to be part of your life through this work.

Revell's mission is to publish books that offer hope and help for meeting life's challenges, and that bring comfort and inspiration. We know that the right words at the right time can make all the difference; it is our goal with every title to provide just the words you need.

We believe in building lasting relationships with readers, and we'd love to get to know you better. If you have any feedback, questions, or just want to chat about your experience reading this book, please email us directly at publisher@revellbooks.com. Your insights are incredibly important to us, and it would be our pleasure to hear how we can better serve you.

We look forward to hearing from you and having the chance to enhance your experience with Revell Books.

The Publishing Team at Revell Books
A Division of Baker Publishing Group
publisher@revellbooks.com

Revell